Urbanization beyond
Municipal Boundaries

DIRECTIONS IN DEVELOPMENT
Countries and Regions

Urbanization beyond Municipal Boundaries

Nurturing Metropolitan Economies and Connecting Peri-Urban Areas in India

THE WORLD BANK
Washington, D.C.

Library of Congress Cataloging-in-Publication Data
Urbanization beyond municipal boundaries : nurturing metropolitan economies and connecting peri-urban areas in India.
       pages cm
   Includes bibliographical references and index.
   ISBN 978-0-8213-9840-1 (alk. paper) — ISBN 978-0-8213-9866-1 (electronic : alk. paper)
   1. Urbanization—India. 2. Suburbs—India. 3. Urban policy—India. 4. Land use, urban—India. 5. India—Economic conditions. 6. Urban economics. I. World Bank.
   HT384.I4U76 2013
   307.760954—dc23

                                                                                                2013000722

Contents

Boxes

Figures

Maps

Tables

Acknowledgments

This report is part of a series of prototypes being piloted under the Urbanization Review, which seeks to build a body of knowledge on urbanization challenges and public policy implications in a variety of country settings. This report was prepared by a core team led by Tara Vishwanath, which included David Dowall, Somik V. Lall, Nancy Lozano-Gracia, Siddharth Sharma, and Hyoung Gun Wang. Henry Jewell, Eugenia Suarez, and Cheryl Young provided research assistance. Important contributions were made by Om Prakash Agarwal in designing the survey on freight costs and the assessment of urban mobility; Augustin Maria and Vasudha Sarda in organizing the case studies on urban policy innovations in India; and Raghu Kesavan and Smita Misra in providing timely feedback and recommendations.

The policy discussion in this report has been framed following extensive discussions with the Planning Commission, Ministry of Urban Development, and Ministry of Housing and Urban Poverty Alleviation. In particular, the team thanks Arun Maira and other members of the committees formed to formulate the urban strategy in the 12th five-year plan, for engaging the team to contribute to this process. The team thanks Ming Zhang, Sector Manager for Urban Development in South Asia, for his overall support and for being an intricate part of the consultations with the government of India in March and December 2011. The concept note and previous drafts of this report benefited from comments from Jan Brueckner, Dean Cira, Indermit Gill, Om Mathur, and Rakesh Mohan. The team worked under the overall supervision of Zoubida Allaoua (Director, Urban and Disaster Risk Management Department, World Bank) and Roberto Zagha (India Country Director, World Bank). The team thanks them for their continuous guidance and support. Bruce Ross-Larson and Jack Harlow at Communications Development edited the report.

About the Authors

Tara Vishwanath is currently a Lead Economist in the Middle East and North Africa (MENA) region's Poverty Reduction and Economic Management group of the World Bank. She leads work in the region on poverty, gender, and impact evaluation. Prior to joining MENA, she led the poverty group in the South Asia region. Before coming to the World Bank, she was a professor in the Department of Economics at Northwestern University and has published widely in international economics journals spanning research topics in economic theory, labor economics, and development. She holds a bachelor's degree in Physics and Statistics, and a doctorate in economics from Cornell University.

Somik V. Lall is a Lead Economist for Urban Development in the World Bank's Urban and Disaster Risk Management Department. He was a core team member of the *World Development Report 2009: Reshaping Economic Geography*, and he was recently Senior Economic Counselor to the Indian Prime Minister's National Transport Development Policy Committee. He currently leads a World Bank program on the Urbanization Review, which provides diagnostic tools and a policy framework for policy makers to manage rapid urbanization and city development. His research interests span urban and spatial economics, infrastructure development, and public finance, with more than 40 publications featured in peer-reviewed journals, edited volumes, and working papers. He holds a bachelor's degree in engineering, master's in city planning, and doctorate in economics and public policy.

David Dowall has worked for the World Bank for the past 27 years, designing urban development projects in more than 200 cities in nearly 50 countries. He was a professor of city and regional planning at the University of California at Berkeley from 1976 to 2012. At Berkeley, he served as the chair of the Department of City and Regional Planning and director of the Institute of Urban and Regional Development, and from 2000 to 2002 he was the chair of the UC Berkeley Faculty Senate. His professional and research work spans strategic and spatial planning, economic development, infrastructure planning, and finance. He has published more than 100 books, academic journal articles, and professional reports. He has a bachelor of science in economics from the University of Maryland, and a master of urban and regional planning and PhD in economics from the University of Colorado.

Nancy Lozano-Gracia is an economist at the World Bank who has worked extensively in the field of economic valuation of urban amenities, such as water, sanitation, and sewerage, as well as goods that are not traded in the market (such as air quality). She is a core team member of the Urbanization Review effort at the World Bank, and her work has covered Brazil, Colombia, India, Turkey, and Vietnam. She holds a doctorate in applied economics from the University of Illinois.

Siddharth Sharma is an economist at the World Bank, which he joined after receiving his PhD in economics from Yale University in 2006. His research interests include: labor markets in developing countries, particularly the impact of labor regulations on firms and households; innovation and productivity of firms in developing countries; and labor and capital mobility and their implications for spatial growth patterns in developing countries. He is currently working in the Africa Department of the World Bank, where he is involved in analytical work on employment, labor markets, and safety nets, including the impact evaluation of a public works project.

Hyoung Gun Wang is an economist in the Urban and Disaster Risk Management Department of the World Bank. He is a core team member of the Urbanization Review flagship study of the World Bank. His research interests are urbanization and urban development, urban and regional economics, spatial economic analysis, economic impacts of infrastructure investment, disaster management methodology, and economic growth at the regional and local levels. His research and work programs have spanned a range of developing countries including Brazil, China, the Democratic Republic of Congo, the Russian Federation, Turkey, and Vietnam, among others. He holds a PhD in economics from Brown University.

Abbreviations

ASI	Annual Survey of Industries
FAR	floor area ratio
FSI	floor space index
GIS	geographic information system
ICT	information and communication technology
JNNURM	Jawaharlal Nehru National Urban Renewal Mission
LARR	Land Acquisition and Rehabilitation and Resettlement
O&M	operation and maintenance
SAR	special administrative region
TDR	transferable development right
UA	urban agglomeration

US$1 = Rs. 55, as of July 2012 exchange rates.

Overview

People and Businesses Are Seeking Metropolitan Suburbs

Identifying options for accommodating urban expansion is gaining importance in India's policy discourse—90 million people joined its urban ranks between 2001 and 2011, and its cities are projected to be home to another 250 million people by 2030. The challenge—as well as the potential opportunity—is that population densities in and around the largest metropolitan areas are extremely high. They are on average 2,450 persons per square kilometer in the 50 kilometer (km) vicinity of the seven largest metropolitan areas (with populations above 4 million in 2001), and a third of India's new towns were "born" in a 50 km neighborhood of existing cities with more than 1 million people.

If these trends are any indication of how the future will unfold, much of India's urbanization challenge will be to transform land use and expand infrastructure in its largest metropolises and their neighboring suburbs—places that are not pristine or greenfield but that already support 9 percent of the country's population and provide 18 percent of the employment on 1 percent of the land area. The challenge so far is that these high population densities have not been supported by commensurate policies and investments to enable residential and commercial development, infrastructure services, and connectivity.

How India's Urbanization Is Managed Affects Productivity, Livability, and Mobility

The rapid growth of metropolitan suburbs is the most striking feature of India's spatial transformation. From an economic efficiency perspective, the important question is whether this move is enhancing productivity by tapping agglomeration economies. Or are agglomeration benefits being stymied by policy distortions, and are there specific reforms that can reduce these inefficiencies? And from a spatial equity perspective—or spatially balanced development—it is important to understand if the benefits of this transformation are spreading geographically—and if there are policies that can support the spread of economic activity, while not impinging on overall economic performance. This report carefully looks at whether public policy is amplifying or dampening the potential productivity gains from urbanization—focusing on policies for land management.

Just as the proximity or density that comes with urbanization can enhance productivity, proximity and density can just as easily transmit disease and enable crime if not properly managed. Has India's urbanization been accompanied by policy measures to provide local public goods and amenities such as clean water, drains, and sewers that can mitigate the potential negative consequences of proximity? These local public goods are central for making cities livable and this report examines the extent to which these are provided across Indian cities, and what the main constraints are in expanding access.

For workers to access jobs and for businesses to access suppliers and markets, a reliable and affordable transport system is needed to enhance urban mobility. Limited transportation options can turn daily commutes in Indian cities into arduous treks, and many people are forced to live in substandard housing and slums to be close to jobs when transport is inaccessible and unaffordable. This report examines the extent of urban mobility across cities—both for people and for products—and identifies areas for improvements.

An assessment of India's urbanization shows overall metropolitan stagnation—the core, suburbs, and peripheries combined—in the concentration of people and jobs. One would have expected to see rapid economic concentration in large metropolitan areas with good market access after India's economic liberalization from the early 1990s, along the lines of what was seen following China's economic liberalization in the 1980s. Similar patterns of increasing economic concentration are also observed in dynamic emerging economies that rapidly urbanized and industrialized. But India's metropolitan areas have not seen discernible gains in economic activity: while the seven largest in the country have the highest concentration of economic activities that benefit from agglomeration economies—such as information and communication technology (ICT) services and high-tech manufacturing—they have, overall, been stagnant in recent years. Between 1993 and 2006, they failed to increase their overall shares in national employment, or even in employment in the above economic activities. International experience—that metropolitan concentration increases until per capita income reaches $7,000–$10,000—suggests that the liberalization of industrial investment decisions in the 1990s should have led to greater economic concentration in India's metropolitan areas.

Explaining Metropolitan Stagnation

India's metropolitan stagnancy is surprising given that the demand for urban agglomerations that can generate productivity spillovers seems to be rising, because India has developed niche markets in ICT services and specialized manufacturing that it trades with the rest of the world. There has also been considerable growth in low-end manufacturing consumed and traded domestically. But land management policies are limiting the extent and intensity at which land can be used and reused by industry, commerce, and housing, severely constraining the carrying capacity of cities. For example, even though the international best practice in cities with limited land (as in Singapore and Hong Kong SAR, China) is to raise the permitted floor space index (FSI)—the ratio of the gross floor area of a building on a lot divided by the area of that lot—to accommodate growth, the Municipal Corporation of Greater Mumbai went the other way, lowering the permitted FSI to 1.33 in 1991. In India's otherwise liberalized economic policy environment, stringent regulations on urban development densities are pushing businesses and people out of urban cores. These constraints on land use are also making housing expensive, pricing out poor and middle-class households from urban centers and increasing commuting costs for workers.

Where do these displaced firms and workers go? To the suburbs, beyond the municipal boundary. And these suburbs are also home to the many new entrants. In fact, at 41 percent, the pace of manufacturing employment growth was fastest in rural areas adjacent to the largest metropolitan areas over 1998–2005 (figure O.1). Even though high-tech and other emerging manufacturing industries are moving away from the cores of metropolitan areas, they are relocating to the immediate suburbs and peripheries of these very cities, not to locations farther away. But although such metropolitan "suburbanization" is a worldwide phenomenon, it usually happens at the middle to advanced stages of development. India's early suburbanization suggests that the overall stagnancy of metropolitan areas is partly because of land management practices that push firms and workers out of the cores.

Figure O.1 Employment Growth in Metropolitan Cores and Peripheries by Sector, 1998–2005

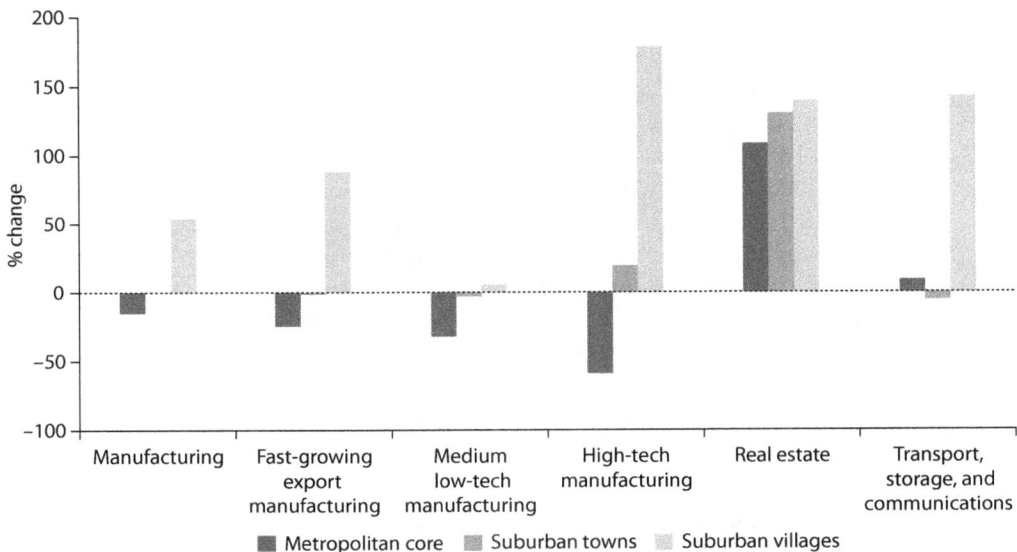

Sources: Ministry of Statistics and Programme Implementation 1998 and 2005.
Note: Metropolitan core includes an area with a radius of 10 km centered on the main metropolis. Suburban towns include urban areas from 10 to 50 km of the metropolitan core, and suburban villages include rural areas in the same vicinity. These figures are averages for the seven largest metropolitan areas (in descending order of population): Mumbai, Delhi, Bangalore, Kolkata, Chennai, Hyderabad, and Ahmedabad.

But the magnitude of suburbanization is not well measured due to a statistical artifact, where places near metropolitan municipalities that look and feel urban are classified as rural. And when you zoom into these places, these "rural" suburban areas beyond the municipal boundaries of metropolitan cities have really high economic growth. In the statistics of urban/metropolitan areas, this looks like stagnation, but looking closer, we see suburbanization (albeit not officially measured).

Thus growth of metropolitan suburbs may well be a reaction to draconian land policy, but this comes with economic costs. In particular, the journey to the suburbs is costly for firms and workers. Transport costs for freight are among the highest nationally between the metropolitan core and its periphery. In addition, infrastructure access and quality for water, electricity, and sanitation is much worse at the urban periphery compared with at the core. These challenges hurt productivity, mobility, and livability. Specific policies and their consequences are now discussed further.

Land Policy Distortions and Infrastructure Shortfalls Reduce Gains from Urbanization

Weak Institutional Foundations for Land Valuation and Transactions Distort the Pace and Shape of Urban Expansion

Urbanization raises demand for land, generating problems when land is scarce in the places it is needed most. Yet India lacks many of the necessary institutions, such as a transparent system to convert land use, a clear definition of property rights, a robust system of land and property valuation, and a strong judicial system for addressing public concerns to facilitate land markets, land transactions, and land use changes.

For example, the process of public land acquisition using the power of eminent domain (compulsory purchase) under the current law, which dates from 1894, is opaque with wide opportunities for corruption. The draft Land Acquisition and Rehabilitation and Resettlement (LARR) bill under discussion seeks to address some of these issues. However, challenges remain because the proposals within the bill do not solve the complex issue of unclear property rights, and there are problems in the way compensation is assigned.

First, India does not have a system to provide independent and reliable valuations of land. Onerous stamp duties, which the LARR bill refers to, have historically created incentives to underreport land and property values—and surveys infrequently update these values. Thus, institutions should be built that improve the information foundations of the valuation process, which would entail training a cadre of appraisers in property valuation, ensuring transparency and consistency in valuation (to get public acceptance), and making information of land values widely accessible (to deter corruption). Without the institutional capacity to help discover and disseminate the value of land, the acquisition process offers considerable scope for undervaluing it.

Second, laws in many countries provide for valuation by independent persons or bodies, rather than by the acquiring authorities. Although the draft bill provides ample opportunity for contesting valuation decisions, greater independence of the valuation expertise along with engagement of affected persons in valuation discussions early in the process could be considered.

While building these institutions is likely to take time, policy makers cannot afford to wait and let the quest for the perfect become the enemy of the better. Alternatives that achieve fair compensation through consultation among affected parties need to be explored in the short term. In addition, stamp duties need to be reduced from their current extremely high rates.

Stringent Regulations on Land Use Induce Sprawl and Escalate Property Prices

Just as valuing land and assigning property rights are challenges for accommodating urban expansion, so are managing densities within cities and finding ways to finance urban expansion and city renewal. But urban regulations such as restrictive FSIs limit densification in Indian cities, capping densities at much below international good practice. A common justification among India's urban planners for keeping urban densities low is that most cities' existing infrastructure systems would collapse if densities were increased. So they argue that existing urban areas should be preserved and development shifted to new towns and suburban industrial estates. Granted, Indian cities have severe infrastructure limits. But these arguments ignore the opportunities of fiscalizing increases in land values to finance higher capacity and higher quality infrastructure networks, and to increase the supply of office space as well as affordable housing for low- and middle-income groups. Density regulations through low FSIs also generate sprawl as development is forced to the periphery of urban areas. In Bangalore, for example, FSI-induced sprawl causes welfare losses of 2–4 percent of household income due to higher commuting costs.

Another striking feature of density regulations is that Indian cities have blanket FSIs that cover large areas—thus missing opportunities to strategically increase densities around infrastructure networks. In fact, "granularity"—or extremely local variations—in FSI design and in coordination of land use to exploit infrastructure placement is the bedrock of good urban planning. Best international practice in cities such as New York, Seoul, and Singapore suggests that planners need to keep in mind that while density should not overwhelm infrastructure capacity, neither should it suboptimally use infrastructure networks.

Suburbanization Is Creating Challenges for Commuting and for Moving Freight

Urban land and building regulations are limiting densities in metropolitan cores and pushing people and firms to the outskirts of large metropolitan areas, and deficiencies in connectivity exacerbate these constraints. A good transport system allows people to make efficient tradeoffs between how much housing and land they consume and its quality, and the distance they travel to work. A weak system, in contrast, heightens the problems of stringent regulations in land markets. People may, for instance, be forced to live in slums if they cannot afford the formal housing market or cannot access cheaper land and housing on the outskirts of cities because of unreliable and unaffordable urban transport.

Congestion presents a major challenge for Indian cities. Narrow roads combined with pervasive growth of private car ownership mean that journey speeds for motorized travel in all cities are barely faster than riding a bicycle. Public transport has not been able to serve the expanding mass of urban commuters, and even though initiatives are under way to enhance its supply, its limited integration with other modes of transport and onerous land use planning are holding down how much it is used.

Just as urban transport services are key for connecting people to jobs in a city, an adequate logistics system and road infrastructure network is needed for city businesses to reach local, regional, and national markets. Market access provides incentives for firms to increase production scale and to specialize. As businesses suburbanize, however, they face increasing market-connection costs. Freight rates between metropolitan cores and their peripheries are as high as Rs. 5.2 per ton-km ($0.12)—twice the national average and more than five times that in the United States. One reason for high transport costs is the use of smaller, older trucks on metropolitan routes. And another is the higher share of empty backhauls (truckers returning without a load) on metropolitan routes. Yet another is that trucks on metropolitan routes clock about 25,000 km annually—just a quarter of what they need to be economically viable. To improve coordination and reduce the cost of metropolitan freight movements, trucking firms could adopt logistics management systems. Or they could form trucking associations.

Spatial Disparities in Access to Basic Services Are Wide

Access to and quality of basic services underpin households' living standards and firms' performance, but India still has a long way to go in providing universal access to such services. Its performance on water availability is disappointing compared with international standards. No major city in India provides more than a small percentage of its population, if any, with continuous water supplies. Yet in Jakarta access is 90 percent, in Manila 88 percent, and in Colombo 60 percent. In Delhi, 59 percent of industrial establishments experience low water pressure. And countrywide differences in access are large, with access to services such as sewerage and drainage worsening as city size decreases. Rural areas suffer from the lowest access levels.

Zooming into the largest seven metropolitan areas also reveals wide spatial variations. These metropolises overall have better access to services than those elsewhere, but wide variations exist between their cores and peripheries. While 93 percent of households in the core have access to drainage, this proportion falls to 70 percent 5 km from the core. Survey data from large cities like Bangalore also confirm access to network services such as piped water is also concentrated in the core, with access levels falling rapidly toward the periphery.

Inefficiencies in delivery and tariffs that do not cover costs jeopardize sustainability and hold back services expansion. In principle, user charges should generate revenues that are at least sufficient to cover operation and maintenance (O&M) costs and asset depreciation, and to yield an adequate return on assets. The operating ratios (O&M cost/revenue) from a small sample of 20 Indian cities paint an alarming picture, however—only a third of water utilities cover their O&M costs. Bhopal, Indore, Kolkata, and Mathura are the worst performers, and financial sustainability is a serious concern for them. Beyond institutional improvements, water utilities must make an effort to achieve 100 percent metered connections. Of the 20 cities, only Bangalore, Coimbatore, Mumbai, and Nashik have at least 70 percent metered connections, Nagpur has 40 percent, and none of the others achieves even 10 percent.

Coordinating Land Policy Reforms with Infrastructure Improvements Can Lay the Foundation for Managing India's Urbanization

Policy Makers Have Highlighted the Centrality of Urban Reforms

As policy makers work toward renewing existing cities and building new towns, they need to make changes to the country's urban planning "license raj." Getting urban planning right is essential for economic prosperity, and the country's policy makers have been grappling with the challenges. The government launched an ambitious program in 2005—the Jawaharlal Nehru National Urban Renewal Mission (JNNURM)—which raised the profile of urban challenges. Box O.1 below discusses lessons from the JNNURM.

Policy Makers Need to Think about Land Market Reforms, Infrastructure Improvements, and Connectivity in an Integrated Manner

Working along these lines, policy makers will be able to inform options for managing economic efficiency and spatial equity tradeoffs associated with India's urbanization. The constraints to agglomeration economies point to inefficiencies in land markets and lack of integration between land use and infrastructure improvements that undercut the potential of urban areas. When policy makers consider building new cities to spread economic opportunities, they should consider that these places are unlikely to flourish if they do not respond to needs of people and businesses—proximity to markets, flexible land markets, and coordinated infrastructure improvements have important roles to play. Policy makers could usefully approach these issues along the following main avenues.

Reduce rigidities in land transactions and land use needed to accommodate urbanization and the development of industry and infrastructure. Land valuation is an integral part of land transactions and local revenue generation, because land values form the basis of property taxes, land sales, and leases. Developed countries have created systems to record and manage information on market transactions that serve as the starting point in valuing land, but India has few of them, and little if any transaction data. Countries where land valuation is successful also have systems that allow for discovery and

Box O.1 What Can Be Learned from the Jawaharlal Nehru National Urban Renewal Mission?

Launched in 2005, the Jawaharlal Nehru National Urban Renewal Mission (JNNURM) has raised the profile of urban challenges among policy makers in India, catalyzing about $24 billion of investments in infrastructure in Indian cities. According to March 2012 data from the Ministry of Urban Development, the mission has approved projects worth $11.2 billion from government-allocated resources. JNNURM envisaged that 23 reforms (11 mandatory and 12 optional) were to be implemented by 67 "mission cities" under JNNURM, including rationalizing stamp duty to no more than 5 percent by 2012, reforming rent control laws (balancing the interests of landlords and tenants), repealing the Urban Land Ceiling and Regulation Act, and recovering operation and maintenance costs from user charges (table BO.1.1).

Has JNNURM helped transform India's urban landscape? Although the intended reforms are laudable and comprehensive, their implementation and impact are unclear. The evaluation design is largely based on self-reported information and tends to focus on inputs and processes rather than outcomes and impacts. To illustrate, we summarize three publicly available studies:

- *Appraisal by the Planning Commission (March 2010), carried out under the mid-term appraisal of the 11th Five-Year Plan.* An expert committee conducted a desk review and pointed out that, while JNNURM had been effective in renewing focus on the urban sector across the country and in catalyzing huge investments in urban infrastructure, it had shown lackluster performance on reforms critical to improving accountability and urban governance. It concluded that capacity building remained a key constraint for effectively implementing infrastructure projects and reform measures, and that most cities had not embraced the notion of integrated urban planning when preparing the city development plans required by JNNURM.

Table BO.1.1 Land and Property Reforms under the Jawaharlal Nehru National Urban Renewal Mission

Reform	States that have passed the reform (of 31 states)	Cities that have passed the reform (of 67 cities)
Rationalization of stamp duty	23	n.a.
Reform in rent control	15	n.a.
Repeal of the Urban Land Ceiling and Regulation Act	30	n.a.
Revision of building by-laws	n.a.	52
Simplification of land conversion laws	n.a.	52
Property title certification system	n.a.	0
Earmarking land for "economically weaker sections" and "low-income groups"	n.a.	54
Computerized process of registration	n.a.	51

Source: http://jnnurm.nic.in/.
Note: n.a. = not applicable.

box continues next page

Box O.1   What Can Be Learned from the Jawaharlal Nehru National Urban Renewal Mission?
(continued)

• *Appraisal by the High Powered Expert Committee for Estimating Investment Requirements for Urban Infrastructure Services (March 2011).* After its own desk review, the Committee concurred with the Planning Commission. It also highlighted the failure of JNNURM to make cities financially sustainable, and noted the limited progress in municipal bonds and public-private partnership arrangements.

• *Independent appraisal by Grant Thornton (May 2011).* The Ministry of Urban Development commissioned an independent mid-term appraisal by consulting firm Grant Thornton, whose findings were included in the ministry's annual update on JNNURM for 2010–11. This appraisal was more rigorous than the previous two and included field visits to 41 cities. The findings also note the lack of municipal capacity, allowing only a minimal role for local bodies in preparing city development plans or detailed project reports. They also point to the absence of environmental and social impact assessments, as well as stakeholder consultations during preparation of detailed project reports.

JNNURM has undoubtedly raised the profile of urban issues among policy makers. But no overall comprehensive impact evaluation study of JNNURM has been carried out so far. The various assessments have highlighted challenges in capacity building and project selection. Given that the 12th Five-Year Plan is looking at options for shaping the second phase of JNNURM, it is important to assess progress to date and to highlight impediments in implementation.

Source: Prepared by the Urbanization Review team.

---

dissemination of land values and that require standardized techniques to enable appraisers to arrive at uniform, transparent, and independent valuations.

While stronger institutions governing land use conversion and land valuation emerge and land markets mature over time, policy makers will need to act in the short to medium terms and may want to look at alternative options. Indian cities could, for example, explore expanding the use of land readjustment for land assembly and infrastructure development. Land readjustment is most commonly used to push out urban boundaries on the periphery of cities, though it may also be used in urban areas for redevelopment.

The premise of land readjustment is to provide public infrastructure at a shared cost to landowners and the municipality. This is achieved by assembling a readjustment area, providing infrastructure and basic services, and then reallocating the land back to the participating private landowners. The reallocation is based either on preadjustment land holdings or land values, but the land amount decreases on the assumption that the value of land has increased through the provision of infrastructure. The land readjustment process allows the land to be developed without the complex transactions that are characteristic of eminent domain. Rather than buying all existing properties commercially or using eminent domain, the government agency can invite owners to participate in the project as capital investors. In return, owners are assured of receiving a property of at least equal value, near their original property, after the area has been developed. Landowners are more amenable to adjustment processes because they can stay where they are, preventing the heavy social and emotional ruptures that often accompany relocation.

Complement these efforts by developing an integrated urban planning process. Infrastructure is needed to support higher densities, and these in turn can increase land values that can be tapped to generate revenues to pay for infrastructure investment. Approaches include levying property taxes and using other land-value capture tools, such as developer charges or impact fees. When focusing on land use regulations and density management policies, international experience suggests that flexibility and granularity are important. In New York, FSIs vary by location and by land use—commercial activities in midtown and downtown have much higher densities than residential areas on the upper east and west sides of Manhattan (map O.1). Also, FSI adjustments and infrastructure investment should go hand in hand—a good example is Singapore, where FSIs vary by not only by location and type of use but by infrastructure availability as well. In areas near metro stations, for example, FSIs are typically higher because the transit system can accommodate increased density and activity resulting from higher FSIs.

The metropolitan area of São Paulo provides an example of how a city can manage density while designing instruments to finance infrastructure. Before 1957, the city's urban legislation imposed constraints on the height of buildings, but these constraints were not really binding. In 1972, FSIs that varied by land use were introduced. Almost 30 years later, a master plan was introduced that changed the way of thinking: building rights became a government allocation. This is today a system of enhanced transferable development rights, where low, basic FSIs are combined with fees that allow building beyond the floor FSIs up to predetermined ceiling FSIs.

In setting out to relax the constraints laid out above, India's policy makers face the choice of embarking on "big bang" reforms in the style of Hong Kong SAR, China; the Republic of Korea; and Singapore—all three of which followed a big push model of managed urbanization with a strong and often intrusive state leading the effort. But this approach could well face high political and social risks in India's polity. A gradual approach may be easier to push through and lead to lower risks, and thus less political and social conflict. One way would be to start by selecting a couple of main streets and several areas around transit stations and developing higher density nodes in those areas, say, by increasing FSIs or selling transferable development rights (or both). India could experiment with different types and combinations of regulations and incentives and see how the market responds.

Build on land policy—the "rules of the game" for improving connectivity and service delivery. Policy makers should think about laying the foundations for

Map O.1 Manhattan's Granular Density Assignments to Leverage Infrastructure Capacity

FSI variations in Manhattan's zoning

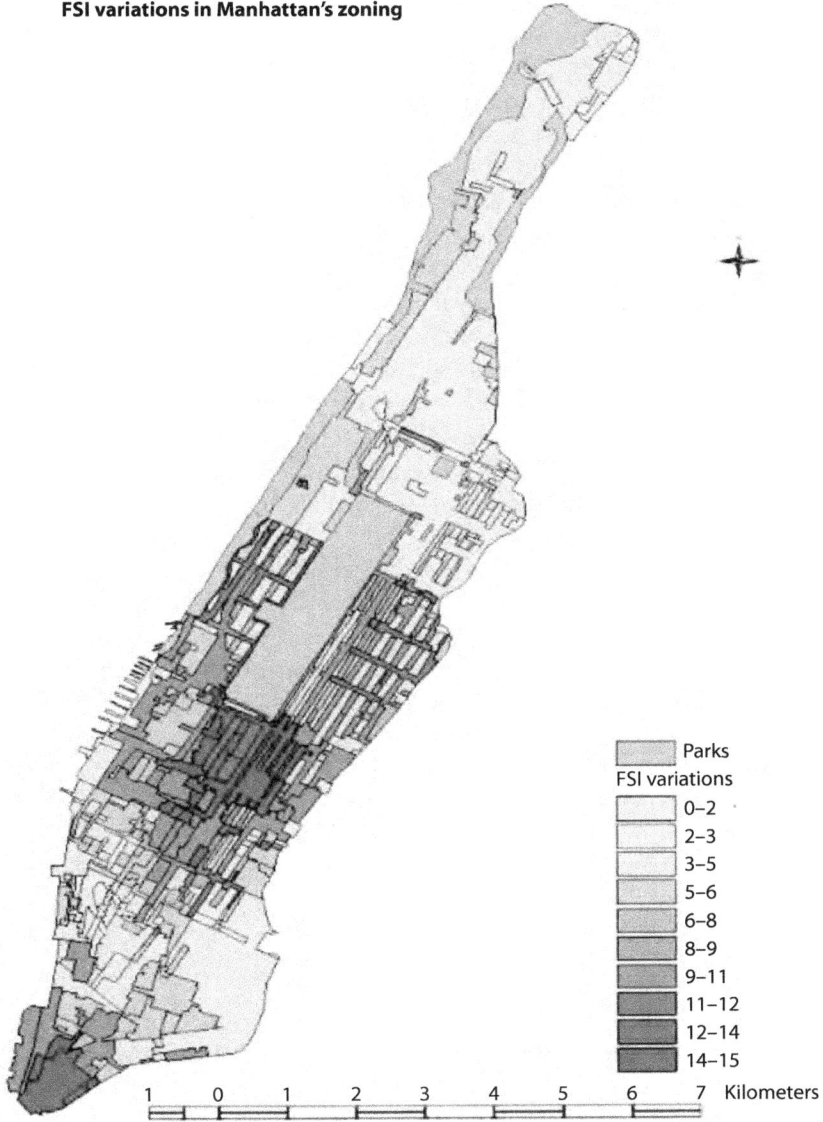

Parks

FSI variations

| 0–2 |
| 2–3 |
| 3–5 |
| 5–6 |
| 6–8 |
| 8–9 |
| 9–11 |
| 11–12 |
| 12–14 |
| 14–15 |

1   0   1   2   3   4   5   6   7   Kilometers

Source: © New York City Planning Department. Reproduced with permission from New York City Planning Department (2011); further permission required for reuse.
Note: In some zones, the floor space index (FSI) might be increased up to two additional units because of bonuses due to plaza, arcades, and the like. In some areas, the permitted FSI might not be reached because of setbacks and plot geometry.

competition and cost recovery in improving services. Cost-covering tariffs are important in improving service sustainability, though in some cases, subsidies may be considered to enhance access for specific groups of the population. In principle, average tariffs should cover costs. When tariffs cover such costs, the right incentives for providers (private or public) to expand and deliver infrastructure services are in place.

Resolve who is responsible for implementing urban reforms in a federal system where national, state, and municipal jurisdictions overlap. Some very local or neighborhood decisions on densification and infrastructure planning are often decided by the state government, and the guidelines on land valuation are concurrently handled by national and state governments, with some input from districts (not necessarily municipalities). Similarly, urban basic services, such as water supply, are often provided by state public health and engineering departments. These approaches pass up potential economies of scale and scope from different service options across settlements with varying densities.

Policy makers should also identify the incentives for coordination among jurisdictions and administrative units, as such coordination allows for service providers to exploit economies of scale. International experience points to the importance of several criteria for designing metropolitan governance structures, including efficiency in exploiting economies of scale and the ability to reduce negative spillovers across municipal boundaries; equity in sharing costs and benefits of services fairly across the metropolitan area; accountability for decision making; and local responsiveness. In India, agencies such as the Bangalore Metropolitan Region Development Authority and the Mumbai Metropolitan Regional Development Authority have been set up to encourage metropolitanwide functional and investment coordination. However, the jury is still out on the effectiveness of these institutions in performing their intended roles, and their ability to manage efficiency, equity, and accountability across the metropolitan area.

International experience also suggests that flexible rules allow cities to respond to changing conditions by reforming interjurisdictional arrangements. Cities like Toronto have clear but flexible rules for responding to the changing pressures of urbanization, adapting these arrangements for service provision. In particular, Toronto moved from a one- to two-tiered government in the 1950s, created a metropolitanwide coordination office in the 1970s, and finally amalgamated municipal arrangements under one "City of Toronto" in the 1980s. In addition, provincewide and sector-specific entities such as the Greater Toronto Transportation Authority have been introduced and reformed over time.

Summary: Integrate Land Policy, Infrastructure Services, and Connectivity

India's policy makers may want to pay immediate attention to three priority areas as they try to harness economic efficiency and manage spatial equity associated with urbanization.

First, to enhance productivity, invest in the institutional and information foundations to enable land and housing markets to function efficiently, while deregulating the intensity of land use in urban areas. This measure would require better coordination between planning for land use and planning for infrastructure, such that densification can be accompanied by infrastructure improvements. An incremental model of experimentation focusing on a few areas—say, around infrastructure corridors and neighborhoods—and then scaling up based on community-level consensus building can help in implementing densification reforms.

Second, to improve livability, rationalize the rules of the game for delivering and expanding infrastructure services, such that providers can recover costs yet reach out to poorer neighborhoods and peripheral areas.

Third, for better mobility, invest in improving connectivity between metropolitan cores and their peripheries, as these are the areas that will attract the bulk of people and businesses over the medium term. Connectivity improvements include investments in network infrastructure and logistics to facilitate movement of goods, while also easing mobility for people.

Land policy, infrastructure services, and connectivity—integrated improvements in this triad can help India reap dividends from improved spatial equity and greater economic efficiency that comes with urbanization.

References

Ministry of Statistics and Programme Implementation. 1998. *Economic Census 1998: All India Report*. Central Statistical Organisation, New Delhi.

———. 2005. *Provisional Results of Economic Census 2005: All India Report*. Central Statistical Organisation, New Delhi.

New York City Planning Department. 2011. *Floor Area Ratio Variations across Manhattan*. City of New York.

CHAPTER 1

Framing India's Urbanization Challenges

Introduction

Much historical and contemporary global evidence shows that spatial transformations accompany countries' structural transformations. Changes in people's decisions on where to live, firms' decisions on where to locate production, and the economic composition of locations—alongside their spatial expansions—are all part of these spatial transformations.

These transformations are occurring rapidly in India. The 2011 census showed that 90 million people were added to India's urban areas since the previous census in 2001. Industrial jobs are concentrating in the suburbs of metropolitan areas, with high-technology and export-oriented manufacturing jobs growing fastest in the periphery of the largest metropolises. These suburbs are delivering economies of agglomeration and specialization, leading the production of goods and services that India trades with the global economy. But the lack of a regional planning framework to integrate peri-urban areas with metropolitan areas is creating challenges for managing fast-expanding urban areas.

Spatial transformations have paced India's impressive economic growth of the past 20 years. In the first decade of this century, GDP grew by 7.2 percent a year, increasing the economic demand for India's urban areas in a manner seen in dynamic emerging economies that have rapidly urbanized and industrialized. For instance, India now has significant global market share in products that often benefit from agglomeration economies and whose global demand is growing at 5–15 percent a year. These products include vehicles, pharmaceuticals, industrial machinery, and electrical and electronic equipment. India's manufactured goods exports were $159 billion in 2008—more than three times its famed information and communication technology (ICT) services exports. Much of India's economic growth has been stimulated through dismantling the "license raj," including rescinding licensing requirements, overhauling public enterprises, scrapping quantitative import restrictions, reducing trade tariffs, and liberalizing rules on foreign direct investment.

How these spatial transformations are managed has implications for both economic efficiency and spatial equity. For economic efficiency, the important question is to identify *where* these transformations are taking place and whether productivity gains through agglomeration economies are being adequately tapped. Put differently: Are agglomeration benefits being stymied by policy distortions, and can specific reforms reduce these inefficiencies? For spatial equity, are the benefits of these transformations spreading geographically? And can policies support the spread of economic activity?

Policy makers in India are trying to balance economic efficiency and spatial equity. In 2005, the Jawaharlal Nehru National Urban Renewal Mission (JNNURM) was launched as the largest ever initiative of the government to address the challenges of urbanization—in hard infrastructure, service delivery improvements, and policy reforms (box 1.1). More recently, the steering committee of the working group on urbanization for the 12th Plan highlights the need to enhance development opportunities in urban areas—making them transit-oriented and compact and offering mixed-income housing. At the same time, the steering committee calls for developing new cities and suburban townships along national transport and industrial corridors, with measures to integrate peri-urban areas.

Policy Framework

To inform options for managing economic efficiency and spatial equity tradeoffs associated with urbanization, this report documents key facts on the pace and patterns of India's spatial transformations, and develops a policy framework to allow policy makers and others to think through issues that can influence the pace, magnitude, and ramifications of these transformations. This report does not provide a blueprint of policy prescriptions nor a checklist of policies for managing urban areas—the focus is to provide fundamental analysis for identifying and resolving key policy distortions.

What does the policy framework examine? Primarily, land policy, and the rules for financing and providing infrastructure services and for maintaining connectivity. This is because the constraints to agglomeration economies point to inefficiencies in land markets and the lack of coordination between land use and infrastructure improvements that stymie the potential of urban areas. When policy makers consider building new cities to spread economic opportunities, they should consider that these places are unlikely to flourish if they do not respond to the needs of people and businesses—proximity to markets, flexible land markets, and coordinated infrastructure improvements have important roles to play.

Land Policy
A sound land policy is needed to ensure both the ease of land transactions and efficient regulations on land use and densification in order to accommodate urbanization and the development of industry and infrastructure.

Box 1.1 What Can Be Learned from the Jawaharlal Nehru National Urban Renewal Mission?

Launched in 2005, the Jawaharlal Nehru National Urban Renewal Mission (JNNURM) has raised the profile of urban challenges among policy makers in India, catalyzing about $24 billion of investments in infrastructure in Indian cities. According to March 2012 data from the Ministry of Urban Development, the mission has approved projects worth $11.2 billion from government-allocated resources. JNNURM envisaged that 23 reforms (11 mandatory and 12 optional) were to be implemented by 67 "mission cities" under JNNURM, including rationalizing stamp duty to no more than 5 percent by 2012, reforming rent control laws (balancing the interests of landlords and tenants), repealing the Urban Land Ceiling and Regulation Act, and recovering operation and maintenance costs from user charges (table B1.1.1).

Has JNNURM helped transform India's urban landscape? Although the intended reforms are laudable and comprehensive, their implementation and impact are unclear. The evaluation design is largely based on self-reported information and tends to focus on inputs and processes rather than outcomes and impacts. To illustrate, we summarize three publicly available studies:

- *Appraisal by the Planning Commission (March 2010), carried out under the mid-term appraisal of the 11th Five-Year Plan.* An expert committee conducted a desk review and pointed out that, while JNNURM had been effective in renewing focus on the urban sector across the country and in catalyzing huge investments in urban infrastructure, it had shown lackluster performance on reforms critical to improving accountability and urban governance. It concluded that capacity building remained a key constraint for effectively implementing infrastructure projects and reform measures, and that most cities had not embraced the notion of integrated urban planning when preparing the city development plans required by JNNURM.

Table B1.1.1 Land and Property Reforms under the Jawaharlal Nehru National Urban Renewal Mission

Reform	States that have passed the reform (of 31 states)	Cities that have passed the reform (of 67 cities)
Rationalization of stamp duty	23	n.a.
Reform in rent control	15	n.a.
Repeal of the Urban Land Ceiling and Regulation Act	30	n.a.
Revision of building by-laws	n.a.	52
Simplification of land conversion laws	n.a.	52
Property title certification system	n.a.	0
Earmarking land for "economically weaker sections" and "low-income groups"	n.a.	54
Computerized process of registration	n.a.	51

Source: http://jnnurm.nic.in/.
Note: n.a. = not applicable.

box continues next page

Box 1.1 What Can Be Learned from the Jawaharlal Nehru National Urban Renewal Mission? *(continued)*

- *Appraisal by the High Powered Expert Committee for Estimating Investment Requirements for Urban Infrastructure Services (March 2011).* After its own desk review, the Committee concurred with the Planning Commission. It also highlighted the failure of JNNURM to make cities financially sustainable, and noted the limited progress in municipal bonds and public-private partnership arrangements.

- *Independent appraisal by Grant Thornton (May 2011).* The Ministry of Urban Development commissioned an independent mid-term appraisal by consulting firm Grant Thornton, whose findings were included in the ministry's annual update on JNNURM for 2010–11. This appraisal was more rigorous than the previous two and included field visits to 41 cities. The findings also note the lack of municipal capacity, allowing only a minimal role for local bodies in preparing city development plans or detailed project reports. They also point to the absence of environmental and social impact assessments, as well as stakeholder consultations during preparation of detailed project reports.

JNNURM has undoubtedly raised the profile of urban issues among policy makers. But no overall comprehensive impact evaluation study of JNNURM has been carried out so far. The various assessments have highlighted challenges in capacity building and project selection. Given that the 12th Five-Year Plan is looking at options for shaping the second phase of JNNURM, it is important to assess progress to date and to highlight impediments in implementation.

Source: Prepared by the Urbanization Review team.

A particularly egregious omission is the lack of a transparent system to convert land use, which stems from an unclear definition of property rights, a nascent system of land and property valuation, and a weak judicial system to address public concerns with land acquisition and conversion. These factors inhibit the functioning of land markets. The draft Land Acquisition and Rehabilitation and Resettlement bill acknowledges the need for land policy reform and puts forward a proposal to support conversion of rural to urban use, but it could still improve the underlying system of valuation and compensation such that it does not distort incentives for existing landowners and developers. However, as land valuation systems and mechanisms to facilitate land assembly develop, it may be useful to consider options for land readjustment, most often used to expand urban boundaries on the periphery of cities. It could also be used for redeveloping urban areas (as is being done in Mumbai's C-Ward).

Urban planning systems across the country limit urban expansion, redevelopment, and modernization. Weak institutional and information foundations governing land markets contribute to urban constraints, with urban plans seeking to preserve the current position by limiting land assembly and freezing the density of development by using a very low floor space index (FSI).[1] These urban regulations create severe shortages of housing and office space in urban areas, driving people and businesses to urban peripheries. A large part of India's challenge with affordable housing stems from rigid rules on densification of urban areas. Best international practice from cities such as New York, Seoul, and Singapore suggests that planners have to keep in mind that while density should not overwhelm infrastructure capacity, neither should it suboptimally use infrastructure networks. In fact, the steering committee or the working group on urbanization for the 12th plan calls for central government incentives to encourage states and cities to pursue strategic densification employing mixed land uses and granular—or extremely local variations—FSIs.

Rules for Infrastructure Services and Connectivity

Building on land policy are the rules for financing and providing infrastructure services, and for maintaining connectivity within and among urban areas. Basic services show spatial disparities in access, as coverage increases with city size, though even with higher access the quality of basic services is low in large cities. There is also a need to work through options for resolving overlapping functions at different levels of government, improving coordination of government and providers, plugging water leakages, and increasing water metering.

As cities expand, the cost of transport increases between the cores of large urban areas and their suburbs, undermining business productivity. The position is made worse by limited options for public transport, reducing labor market opportunities, particularly for poor households. The connectivity challenge is further exacerbated by the rapid growth of private motor vehicles, which adds to congestion and deteriorates air quality.

Other Focus Areas

Drawing on international experience, this report provides options—relevant and actionable in India—for policy innovations. These options should help improve the effectiveness of urban investments and prioritize investments across the urban system. The diagnostics here have been discussed with a wide range of stakeholders in India, including the Planning Commission, the ministries of urban development and of housing and urban poverty alleviation, research institutes, and think tanks. These consultations have highlighted the importance of policy reform in land and urban planning, infrastructure services, and connectivity as the foundations to support urban development. The examination of several policy distortions—especially as they relate to land and infrastructure—in this report was motivated by the discussions during these consultations. The policy distortions identified and potential solutions offered here are consistent with the recommendations laid out by the Steering Committee on Urbanization for the 12th Plan.

Focusing on key policy issues, this report complements recent efforts by Indian government committees and private entities to identify the size and sectoral spread of investments needed to finance urban development. McKinsey Global Institute (2010) suggests that India spends $17 per capita a year on urban infrastructure, whereas most benchmarks would suggest $100 is required. The investment needed for building urban infrastructure in India over the next 20 years is estimated at $1.2 trillion, with another $1 trillion for operating expenditures. HPEC (2011) also highlighted the infrastructure deficit in urban areas, pointing to investment needs of $800 billion in the next 20 years, with more than 40 percent for transport improvements. Similar sectoral directions are provided in McKinsey's report, which calls for 350–400 km of public transit including metros and subways to be built every year, an annual amount more than 20 times what India has put in place in the past decade. Finally, the steering committee has identified that Rs. 290,694 ($53 billion) are needed from the central government to support urban investment over 2012–17.

This report does not cover a few seemingly important issues. Notably, it does not provide projections of the spatial distribution of jobs or people over the next 20 years, nor does it predict where new towns will emerge. This is partly because some of these projections have been made in recent reports, and partly because projections of urban growth or the spatial evolution of countries—unlike demographic projections—are economic projections and endogenous to policy and investment choices (HPEC 2011; McKinsey Global Institute 2010). Nor does it delve into the system of intergovernment transfers or provide a review of municipal finances and options for borrowing. World Bank (2011) provides a broad treatment of these issues.

Implementing Policy Reforms

In implementing reforms, policy makers face the choice of embarking on "big bang" reforms in the manner of Hong Kong SAR, China; the Republic of Korea; and Singapore—all three of which followed a big push model of managed urbanization with a strong and often intrusive state leading the effort. However, this approach could face high political and social risks in India's polity. Another option, which may be more appropriate to India's democratic and federal system, is to pursue an incremental model of experimentation focusing on a few areas—say, around infrastructure corridors and neighborhoods—and then scaling up based on community-level consensus building. This will also allow for learning from alternative approaches and lead to local capacity building.

A related question arises on who is responsible for implementing urban reforms in a federal system where national, state, and municipal government jurisdictions overlap. Some very local or neighborhood decisions on densification and infrastructure planning are often decided by the state government, and the guidelines on land valuation are concurrently handled by national and state governments, with some input from districts (not necessarily municipalities). Similarly, urban basic services such as water supply are often provided by state public health and engineering departments, passing up potential economies of scale and scope from different service options across settlements with varying densities.

Beyond implementation challenges associated with vertical coordination, India's rapidly increasing spatial footprint—or suburbanization of urban areas—is creating a disconnect between what is "urban" and what is "municipal," calling for metropolitanwide horizontal coordination. International experience points to several criteria for designing metropolitan governance structures, including efficiency in exploiting economies of scale and the ability to reduce negative spillovers across municipal boundaries; equity in sharing costs and benefits of services fairly across the metropolitan area; accountability for decision making; and local responsiveness. Agencies such as the Bangalore Metropolitan Region Development Authority and the Mumbai Metropolitan Region Development Authority have been set up to encourage metropolitanwide functional and investment coordination. However, the jury is still out on the effectiveness of these institutions in performing their intended roles, and their ability to manage efficiency, equity, and accountability across the metropolitan areas.

Structure of the Report

The report is organized into three chapters:

- Chapter 2 looks at the pace and patterns of India's urbanization, providing a 100-year perspective on demographic shifts and a 20-year perspective on the spatial distribution of jobs across India's portfolio of settlements. The review is based on a careful, spatially detailed analysis of data from economic and demographic censuses, annual surveys of industry, national sample surveys, and special surveys of freight transport. This chapter provides diagnostics on whether Indian industry is adequately exploiting agglomeration economies and whether there are hints of specific barriers to the natural tendency of standardized industry to reshuffle from large metropolitan areas to smaller urban areas.

- Chapter 3 examines specific policy issues and investment bottlenecks that are curbing the pace and benefits of urbanization in India. The policy issues relate to land markets and housing, connectivity (within and between cities), and access to basic services. The purpose of this analysis is to unravel the specific distortions that may be preventing India from reaping the entire range of benefits of urbanization.

- Chapter 4 provides some options for policy reform, distilling lessons from relevant international experience. It provides options for establishing the "rules of the game" that can define the workings of land and property markets as well as coordination of land use and infrastructure in cities. This chapter also provides a framework for policy makers to identify the role of regulatory and price reform in expanding infrastructure services and to make investments that enhance capacity.

Note

1. FSI is the ratio of the gross floor area of a building on a lot divided by the area of that lot (see figure 3.1).

References

HPEC (High Powered Expert Committee). 2011. *Report on Indian Urban Infrastructure and Services.* Government of India, New Delhi.

McKinsey Global Institute. 2010. *India's Urban Awakening: Building Inclusive Cities, Sustaining Economic Growth,* by Shirish Sankhe, Ireena Vittal, Richard Dobbs, Ajit Mohan, Ankur Gulati, Jonathan Ablett, Shishir Gupta, Alex Kim, Sudipto Paul, Aditya Sanghvi, and Gurpreet Sethy. New Delhi.

World Bank. 2011. "Developing a Regulatory Framework for Municipal Borrowing in India." World Bank, South Asia Urban Development Department, Washington, DC.

CHAPTER 2

India's Urban Evolution:
A Historical Outlook

Urban Geography: A 100-Year Perspective

India has enjoyed impressive economic progress over the past 20 years, and GDP grew by 7.2 percent a year in the first decade of the century. Much of this progress has been stimulated by dismantling the license raj, including removing licensing requirements, overhauling public enterprises, eliminating quantitative import restrictions, reducing tariffs, and liberalizing rules on foreign direct investment. But, surprisingly, the fast economic growth has not been matched by a commensurate pace of urbanization: estimates from India's Central Statistical Organisation indicate that the urban share of national net domestic product crept up by only 0.32 percentage points (from 51.7 percent) between 1999/2000 and 2004/05, a time when the national economy was expanding rapidly.

In most countries, economic growth and industrialization have been accompanied by steadily rising urbanization, reaching levels of around 75 percent for the most advanced economies. India's urbanization trajectory appears to be lower than in other developing economies, based on official statistics (figure 2.1). This anomaly is particularly ironic as the Indian subcontinent was home to some of the earliest urban settlements in human history, Mohenjo-Daro and Harappa, which are known to have arisen around 5,000 years ago.

India's growth without significant urbanization poses a major puzzle: between 1980 and 2011, the urban share of the overall population rose from just 23 to 32 percent, while China's more than doubled from 20 to 45 percent. Although slow spatial transformation would suggest that India is not reaping productivity benefits from urban agglomeration economies, the country's economic performance is consistent with that of dynamic emerging economies that have rapidly urbanized and industrialized. As said, India has significant global market share in many fast-growing products that generally benefit from agglomeration economies. So how does rapid economic transformation square with the slow pace of urbanization? Are specific policy distortions and investment shortfalls dampening agglomeration economies?

Figure 2.1 Urbanization and Development—Developed and Developing Countries, plus India, 1800–2010

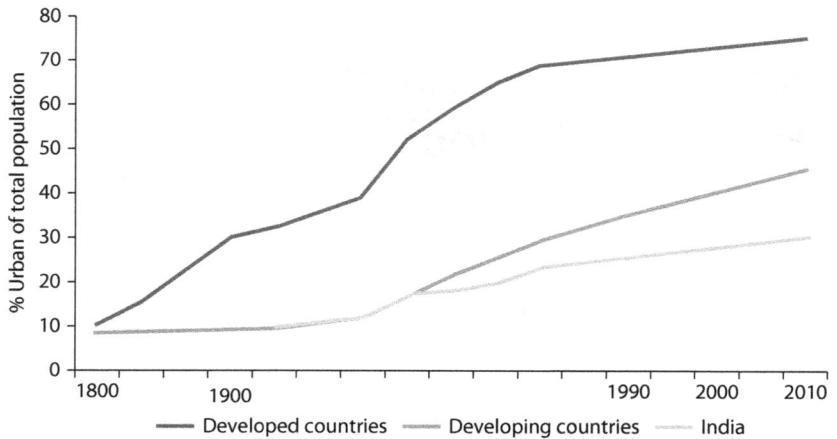

Source: Bairoch 1988; "World Urbanization Prospects, the 2011 Revision," United Nations Department of Economic and Social Affairs, http://esa.un.org/unup.

How India Defines Urban Areas

Before looking at policy and investment, one must appreciate that India's stringent definitions of "urban"—not updated in 50 years—are likely to create a statistical artifact (box 2.1). In fact, the Agglomeration Index—a globally comparable measure of urbanization using population density (150 people per square kilometer), the minimum size of a large urban center (50,000 inhabitants), and travel time to that urban center (60 minutes)—shows India to be 52 percent urbanized.[1]

Downward bias on India's urban statistics is also caused by delays in redrawing municipal boundaries as these areas expand. For instance, while 2,774 additional settlements exhibited urban characteristics between 2001 and 2011, only 147 have official urban status. The rest have urban characteristics but are not considered urban for policy purposes. This poses a real measurement challenge as the edges of large metropolitan areas have attracted many people and businesses over the past 20 years but most of them are officially classified rural. In fact, rapid growth of metropolitan edges—suburbanization—is the most striking feature of India's spatial transformation.[2]

A Stable Urban System

India's urban structure has been fairly stable over the past 100 years. The share of the urban population in cities of more than 1 million rose from 27 percent in 1901 to 38 percent in 2001. The urban population is fairly scattered (map 2.1). The seven largest metropolitan areas with more than 4 million people (in 2001) are dispersed across the country[3]; the same holds for other city groups that are functionally linked to cities higher up the urban hierarchy. This pattern contrasts with China, where the majority of large cities are in the east, medium-size cities in the center, and small cities dispersed in the west (box 2.2).

Box 2.1   Official Classification Imposes Downward Bias on Urban Statistics

India uses more demanding criteria than most countries to define urban. Since its 1961 census, it has used the following three: a population of 5,000 or more, a density of at least 1,000 persons per square mile (or 400 per square kilometer), and at least 75 percent of workers engaged in nonagricultural employment (this was further narrowed in 1981 to male workers only).

Yet even at the 1961 census, some officials were recommending three categories—urban, suburban, and rural—in recognition that an urban/rural dichotomy was too simple. More recently in the 1991 census, areas lying just outside the statutory limits of a town but not satisfying the criteria on their own to qualify as urban were termed "outgrowths." Given these consequences of India's narrow definition of urban, the official census statistics for India's urbanization should, by international standards, be considered a lower bound.

An additional downward bias on India's urban statistics comes from tardy procedures in redrawing municipal boundaries as cities and towns expand. Subnational governments have to notify such changes through the office of the deputy commissioner or district magistrate to invite any objections to such changes.

Also, local politicians may not want to be classified as urban, because, once designated a statutory town, the local government may lose preferential treatment in intergovernment transfers and public resources. An additional complication is that official urban population statistics may not be consistent between states, because some state governments use their powers more than others to designate urban areas.

A more consistent and accurate method is required to count India's true urban population.

Source: Prepared by the Urbanization Review team.

The limited coastal urban concentration has a bearing on how Indian industry trades globally—and is driven partly by underinvestment in intercity transport that could enable several coastal cities to develop. Much of India's transport network is inherited from the colonial era, and people are still concentrated near these historical infrastructure links. In 1901, 82 percent of India's urban population lived within 10 km of a railroad, and 85 percent in 2001 (figure 2.2). The railroad network today looks pretty much as it did in the 1930s (see table A.3). Dedicated freight corridors are now being planned for railways, and the National Highway Development Program is opening new areas for development. These investments should have a heavy bearing on the spatial distribution of people in the future.

This slow expansion of infrastructure networks in India is likely to have trapped people in some places when economic opportunities have been generated elsewhere. Countries such as the Republic of Korea, in contrast, matched new demand with infrastructure growth, allowing for a well-developed system of cities over several decades (box 2.3).

Map 2.1 Spatial Distribution of Urban Agglomerations and Towns by Size, 2001

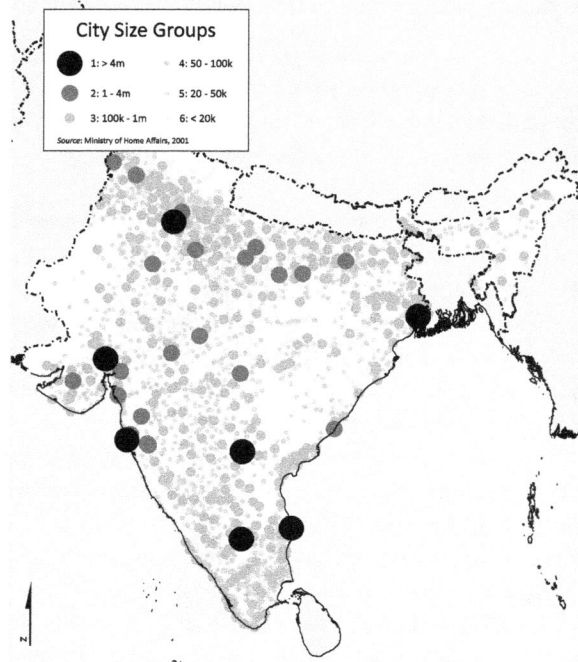

Source: © Ministry of Home Affairs, India. Reproduced with permission from Ministry of Home Affairs (2001); further permission required for reuse.

Economic Geography: A 20-Year Horizon

India's industrial geography has evolved following liberalization in the early 1990s—but policy distortions and infrastructure shortfalls are undermining performance. While entrepreneurs are choosing locations most conducive for profitability—India's largest metropolitan areas that have good access to domestic and international markets—overregulated land markets are limiting urban densities and pushing up prices for land and property. As people and jobs suburbanize, they face high transport costs in maintaining contact with the core: short-distance freight costs are around Rs. 5 per ton-km, twice the average in 2010 and twice China's average in 2002.[4] Suburbanization also poses challenges for urban mobility, increasingly constrained by public transport's limited role. Basic services are weak, and metropolitan peripheries fare poorly on access and quality.

Such overregulated land markets, poor interregional and intra-urban connectivity, and inadequate public services are dampening gains from urbanization. (These points are discussed further in chapter 3. Before that, the next two sections look at recent patterns of economic concentration, and changes in those patterns.)

Metropolitan Dominance in Economic Activity

In economic concentration measured by employment, using the administrative definition of urban areas, manufacturing is evenly split between rural (52 percent)

Box 2.2 Dispersed Urban Settlements in India, Coastal Concentration in China and the United States

Map B2.2.1 presents spatial profiles of urban footprints (or land use) for India, China, and the United States, generated using remotely sensed 2001 data from the MODIS satellite, at 500-meter spatial resolution.

For India, it shows relative concentration along major rivers like the Ganges and Godavari, though the footprint is more spatially dispersed than in China and the United States, which show dense concentration of urban areas along the coasts. Spatially, urban expansion in India is more inward-oriented, while that in China and the United States is more outward-oriented.

Map B2.2.1 Urban Footprints: India, China, and the United States, 2001

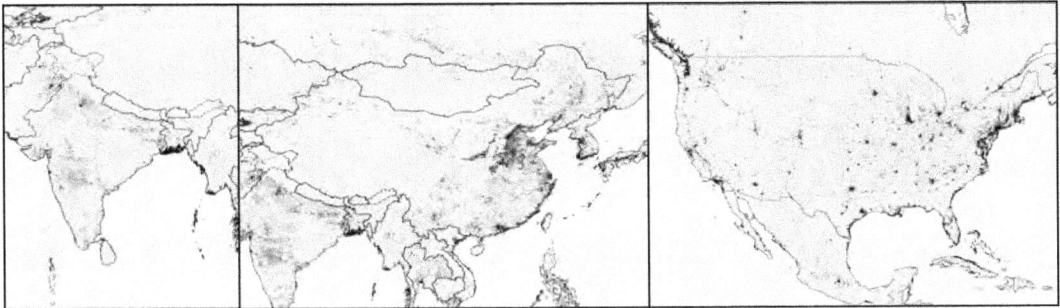

Source: Produced using GIS data by Schneider, Friedl, and Potere 2009.

Figure 2.2 Share of Urban Population within 10 Kilometers of a Railroad, 1901–2001

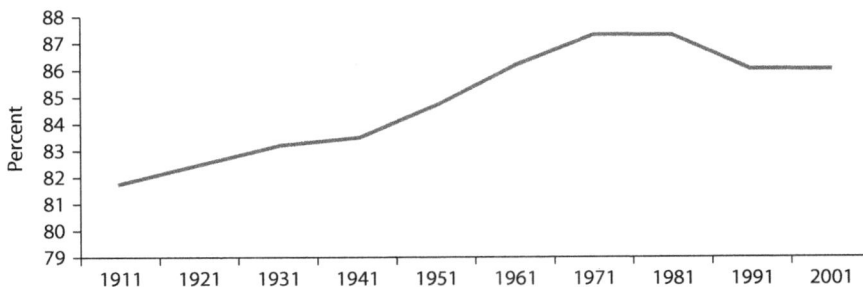

Source: Urbanization Review team calculations, based on various censuses.

and urban (48 percent) areas (table 2.1). However, more technology-intensive goods are produced in urban areas: medium high tech (64 percent) and high tech (58 percent).[5] The urban concentration is also much higher for fast-growing export manufactures (63 percent), and overwhelming for ICT services (95 percent).[6] Appendix B discusses the data sources and processing techniques used in the analysis.

Box 2.3 The Republic of Korea Made Strategic Decisions to Expand Infrastructure Networks, Enabling New Towns to Develop

For the last few decades, the Republic of Korea's urban expansion has been concentrated along transport corridors that link the largest metropolitan cities of Seoul in the northwest and Busan in the southeast (map B2.3.1). Manufacturing followed the same spatial path, from initial concentration in core urban centers and expanding to their suburban areas around the transport network (maps B2.3.2 and B2.3.3).

Map B2.3.1 Spatial Distribution of Cities by Size, 1960, 1980, and 2005

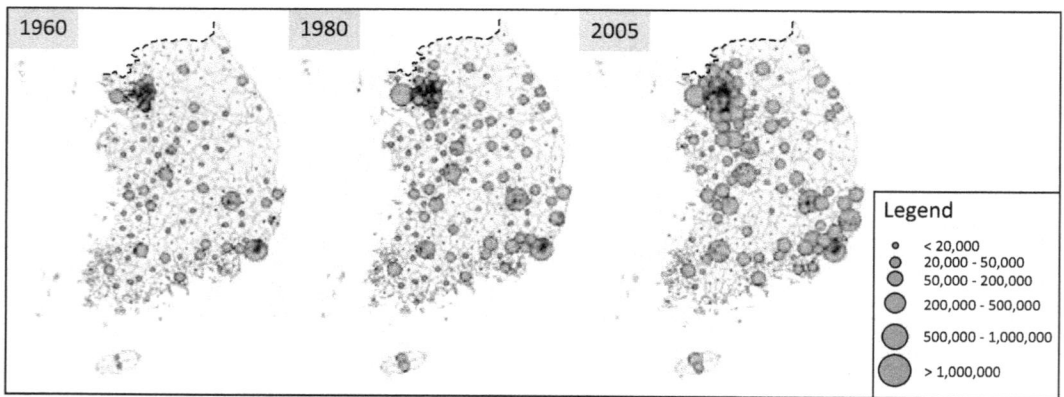

Source: World Bank 2011.

Map B2.3.2 Change in Share of Manufacturing Employees, 1960, 1980, and 2005

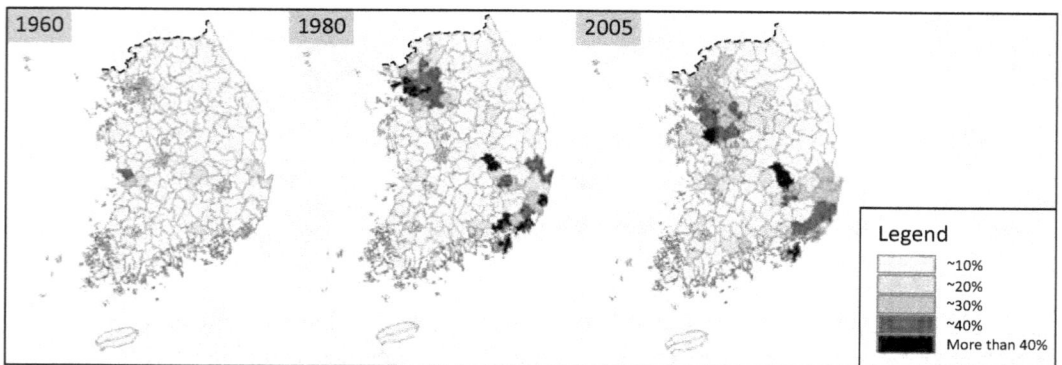

Source: World Bank 2011.

box continues next page

Box 2.3 The Republic of Korea Made Strategic Decisions to Expand Infrastructure Networks, Enabling New Towns to Develop *(continued)*

Map B2.3.3 Change in Intercity Connectivity, 1970, 1980, and 2010

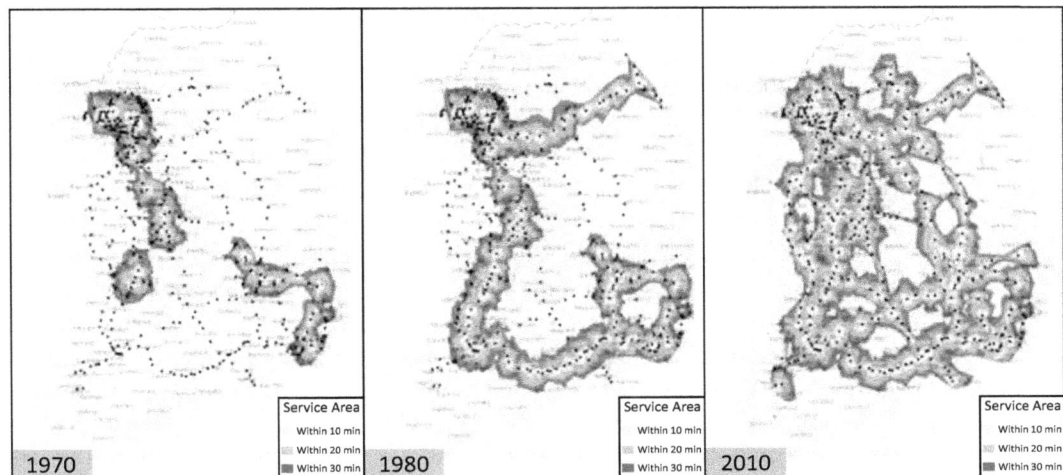

Source: World Bank 2011.
Note: Change of areas by arrival time to the closest expressway interchange, within 10, 20, or 30 minutes.

Table 2.1 Economic Activity across the Portfolio of Settlements

	City size							
	More than 4 million	1–4 million	100,000–1 million	50,000–100,000	20,000–50,000	Fewer than 20,000	Urban total	Rural total
a. Population in 2001 (millions)	65	42.2	89.1	27.8	35.2	26.8	286	743
National share (%)	6.3	4.1	8.7	2.7	3.4	2.6	27.8	72.2
b. Number of workers, 2005 (millions)	13.1	6.7	14.2	4.7	5.7	3.2	47.6	48.3
National share (%)	13.7	7.0	14.8	4.9	5.9	3.3	49.6	50.4
Economic participation rate (b/a) (%)	20.2	15.9	15.9	16.8	16.1	11.9	16.6	6.5
Percentage of labor force engaged in the economic activity								
Agriculture and forestry	0.5	0.7	2.0	1.0	1.3	0.9	6.5	93.5
Fishing	1.1	0.8	6.0	2.6	2.1	2.5	15.1	84.9
Mining and quarrying	4.2	4.2	9.2	3.2	4.2	4.3	29.4	70.6
Manufacturing	14.1	7.7	13.4	4.5	5.3	2.8	47.9	52.1
Low tech	23.1	10.3	15.2	5.4	5.6	3.2	62.9	37.1
Medium low tech	13.0	7.0	13.5	4.8	5.5	2.9	46.6	53.4
Medium high tech	15.1	8.5	12.3	3.5	4.4	2.5	46.3	53.7
High tech	20.0	14.4	14.6	5.9	5.8	3.0	63.7	36.3
Fast-growing exports	22.5	11.6	12.0	3.6	6.9	1.9	58.4	41.6
ICT services	54.5	13.3	20.0	2.5	3.1	1.2	94.6	5.4

Sources: Ministry of Home Affairs 2001; Ministry of Statistics and Programme Implementation 2005.

The findings on the spatial patterns of industrial composition mirror insights from the product cycle theory. That theory postulates that new high-tech products are developed and initially produced in large cities, and as production technologies are standardized, production relocates to specialized small cities where production costs are lower. We examine this in India using the location quotient, a measure of geographic concentration of an industry, defined as the ratio of a location's share of the industry's employment to its share of national employment. Values above (less) than 1 indicate that the location is relatively more (less) specialized in the industry than the national average. Small towns are more specialized in agriculture, fishing, and mining activities (relative to the urban average; see table A.16).

Manufacturing, overall, does not show any specialization in a certain size of city group. But within manufacturing, as expected, high-tech industries are specialized in the seven largest cities, and medium low– or medium high–tech industries are more densely specialized in the second-tier cities of 1–4 million people. Fast-growing export manufactures and, more distinctly, information and communication technology (ICT) services are specialized only in the largest cities (map 2.2). The service sector shows higher specialization in the largest cities in two subsectors—transport, storage, and communications and real estate, renting, and business activities. Small towns of fewer than 20,000 people show quite high specialization in utility services of electricity, gas, and water

Map 2.2 Employment Distribution in High-Tech Manufacturing and ICT Services, 2005

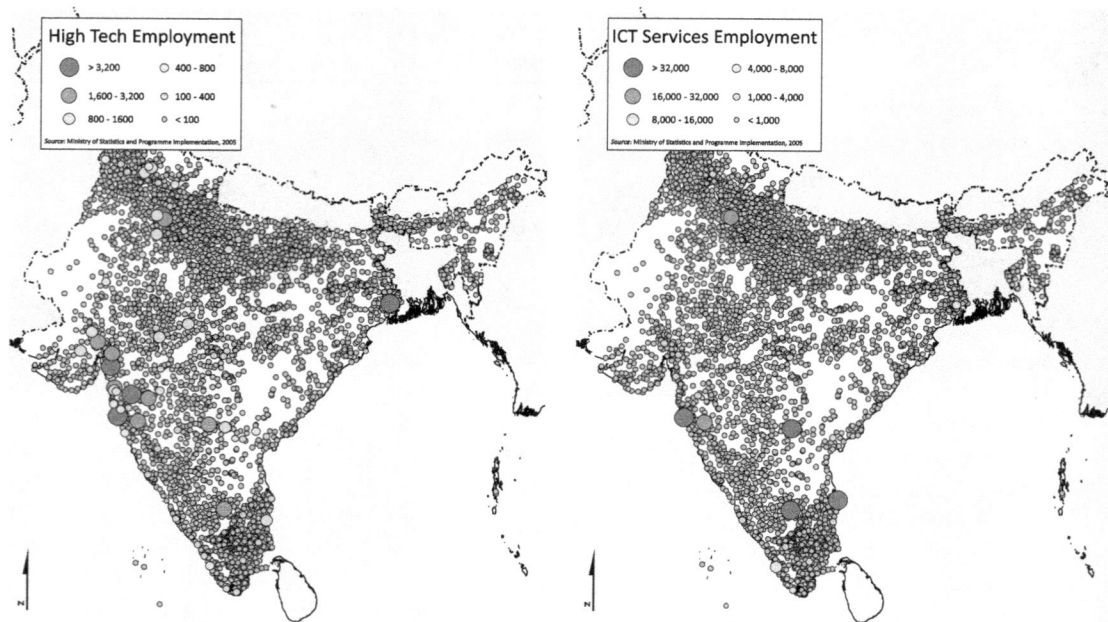

Source: © Ministry of Statistics and Programme Implementation, India. Reproduced with permission from Ministry of Statistics and Programme Implementation (2005); further permission required for reuse.

supply. Financial services, often concentrated in the largest cities, are relatively evenly dispersed.

The corresponding location quotients for China, Brazil, and the United States suggest that manufacturing is initially concentrated in large cities (as in China), disperses across the urban system (as in Brazil) as economic development progresses, and finally becomes specialized in small cities and towns at a mature stage (as in the United States; see table A.16). Given their levels of development, we expect India to resemble China more than it does Brazil or the United States. But even as India resembles China in some aspects (such as the dispersed location of financial industries), some structural differences between them emerge.

India's overall manufacturing activity is dispersed across the urban system, given its early stage of development (despite some specialization of high-tech manufacturing in large cities). In contrast, China's cities are highly specialized in manufacturing. Also, basic public services in large cities in India, like health, education, social security, and public administration, are significantly underinvested relative to China (and even more so than in the United States). For example, the location quotient of education employment in India's largest cities is 0.85, less than the national average, and much less than in China (1.16) and the United States (1.40).

Because the above analysis used a stringent administrative definition of urban areas, the analysis was redone with an alternative definition, in which the unit of analysis is the effective "economic shadow" of metropolitan areas around their urban nucleus—that is, all towns and rural tehsils[7] within a specified distance of the city center.

Firms' data in towns for the urban sector and tehsil data for the rural sector were extracted from the 2005 economic census.[8] These town and tehsil locations ("centroids") were then geo-referenced in a GIS data format, and the straight-line (Euclidean) distance from each town or tehsil to the city center computed. The objective was to rework the specialization analysis using a definition of a metropolitan city as the area within a 50 km radius of the city center, a distance chosen as a default distance as it would be around the distance that can be traveled in two hours or less, approximating the extent of economic interactions within an urban area. Of course, this distance could be increased with better transport networks or lowered with worse congestion. Although illustrative only, this 50 km buffer reveals some interesting findings.

The key finding is that population and economic activity are highly concentrated around the seven largest cities and their neighboring areas, more so than with the administrative definition. The 50 km economic shadow of these seven cities covers only 1.1 percent of the land area in India but holds 92 million people—in 2001, 9 percent of the total, a quarter of the urban population, and less than 3 percent of the rural population. The population density is 2,451 people per square kilometer, almost eight times as high as the national average. The share of the urban population in this land area is 78 percent, well above the national average of 28 percent (table 2.2).

The first ring buffer up to 50 km of the center of these seven largest cities contains 18 percent of national employment (see table A.9). As expected, agriculture,

Table 2.2 Location of Population in Multiple Ring Buffers for the Seven Largest Cities, 2005
%, unless otherwise indicated

	Radius from the center						
	Less than 50 km	50–100 km	100–200 km	200–300 km	300–450 km	More than 450 km	Total
Land area	1.1	3.3	11.9	16.7	24.7	42.2	100.0
Total population	8.9	4.5	13.7	16.3	20.6	36.0	100.0
Urban population	24.9	3.6	12.9	17.2	19.2	22.1	100.0
Rural population	2.8	4.9	14.0	15.9	21.1	41.3	100.0
Population density (per sq. km)	2,451	427	364	306	262	269	315
Urbanization rate[a]	77.7	22.4	26.2	29.4	25.9	17.1	27.8

Sources: Ministry of Home Affairs 2001; Ministry of Statistics and Programme Implementation 2005.
a. Ratio of urban population to total population.

fishing, and mining are much less intense closer to the urban core, while as in other countries, business services are concentrated within a 50 km radius, with 29 percent of national employment. But even with this less stringent definition of urban areas, manufacturing as a whole does not show a noticeable concentration.

However, this alternative definition reconfirms the finding that more sophisticated industries cluster around large cities. For example, the employment share within 50 km of the seven city centers increases from 17 to 36 percent as one moves up the technology ladder from low tech to high tech (see table A.10). A significant presence of high-tech industries is observed even in administratively defined "rural" areas within the 50 km economic shadow. Also striking is that 64 percent of national ICT services jobs fall within this shadow. Of the nation's fast-growing export manufacturing jobs, 30 percent are also concentrated in this shadow.

Slow Pace of Economic Concentration

Patterns of economic concentration have, obviously, changed over time. Cross-country experience suggests a constant churn in location patterns between and within industries: some types of firms agglomerate, others disperse. Young industries—or those that recently experienced a major technological advance—locate in large cities to maximize learning spillovers. Then, as they mature and other factors such as cheap labor or land start to matter more, they tend to disperse. This dispersion is enabled by reliable transport networks ensuring connectivity and market access. In India, trends indicate that industries that exhibit agglomeration economies remain in the vicinity of large cities.

We may consider, for instance, how the spatial concentration of ICT services employment evolved between 1998 and 2005 (figure 2.3). The big seven metropolitan cores and surrounding districts remained specialized in ICT services, with a location quotient near 3 in both periods. Other million-plus cities showed an emerging specialization in ICT, with their location quotient crossing the critical threshold of 1 over the same period.[9] Thus, while some dispersion

Figure 2.3 Trends in Spatial Concentration of ICT Services Employment, 1998 and 2005

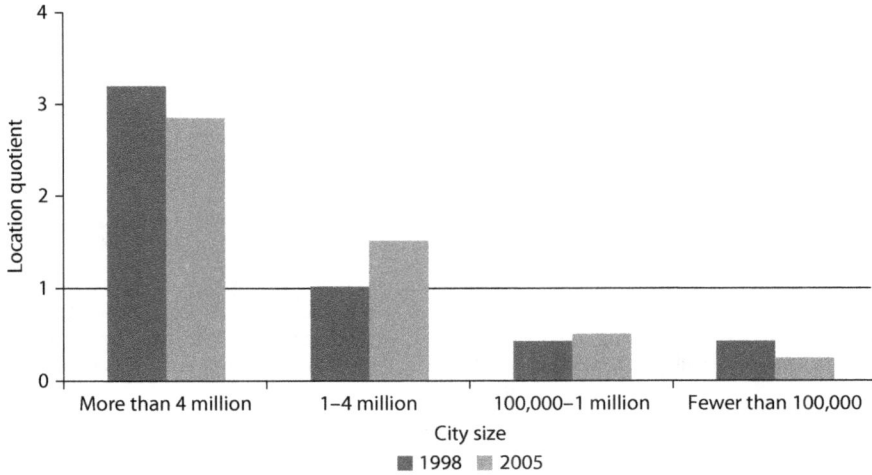

Sources: Ministry of Statistics and Programme Implementation 1998 and 2005.

occurred as India's ICT industry matured, agglomeration forces were still strong enough to limit this dispersion to million-plus cities. Since all other districts had a location quotient well below 1 and did not show a significant upward trend, the ICT industry may well remain concentrated in the largest cities for some time.

The big seven and other million-plus cities specialize in high-tech and high-export growth manufacturing industries, and the data hint at increasing specialization in the big seven. In high-tech manufacturing, a clear trend is the persistence of spatial specialization, with no sign of dispersion to smaller cities (figure 2.4).

While India largely conforms to international experience in the patterns of spatial specialization, the slow pace of change is surprising. As leading areas of concentration grow beyond a certain size and density, the economies from agglomeration are outweighed by "diseconomies" of agglomeration—such as congestion—suggested by rising rents and wages. The slowdown and subsequent partial reversal of spatial concentration normally happens at a late stage of development. For France, this turning point was at a per capita GDP of $7,000. Even more typical are Canada and the Netherlands, at about $10,000. In Japan during its post–World War II industrialization, the concentration in its leading area of greater Tokyo continued increasing until 1970. In China, the largest cities are still growing in population and GDP faster than other cities in the country.

If these trends provide a broad benchmark, India, at income levels of less than $1,500—or well below $7,000–10,000—should expect economic concentration to increase in the years to come. It is here that India puzzles. The left panel in figure 2.5 shows, as expected, that districts in all cities with more than 1 million people accounted for an outsized share of total formal manufacturing employment. But the conundrum is that concentration in those two categories

Figure 2.4 Trends in Spatial Concentration Location Quotient of High-Tech and of High-Export Growth Manufacturing Industries, 1993 and 2006

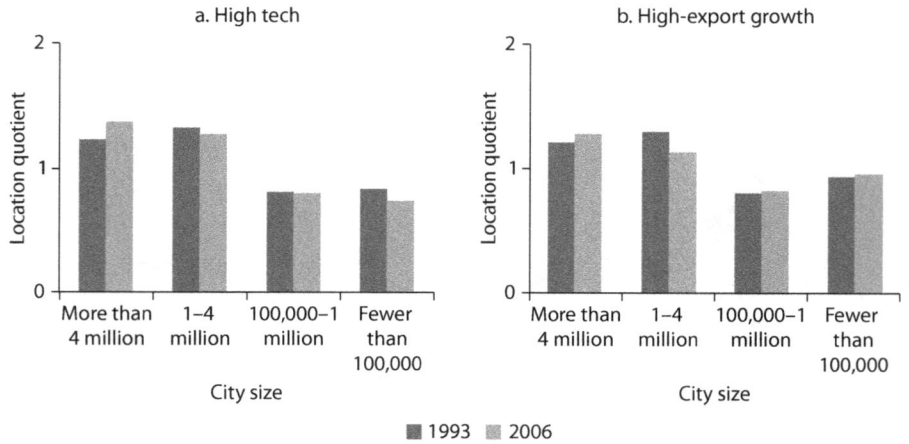

a. High tech

b. High-export growth

1993   2006

Sources: Ministry of Statistics and Programme Implementation 1994 and 2007.
Note: These trends are based on district total fixed capital in factories belonging to the respective industries, as estimated in the Annual Survey of Industries reports. Trends based on district total employment in these factories are similar. Trends are limited to the formal manufacturing sector and based on total fixed capital in factories.

Figure 2.5 Spatial Trends in Total Formal Manufacturing and Services Employment

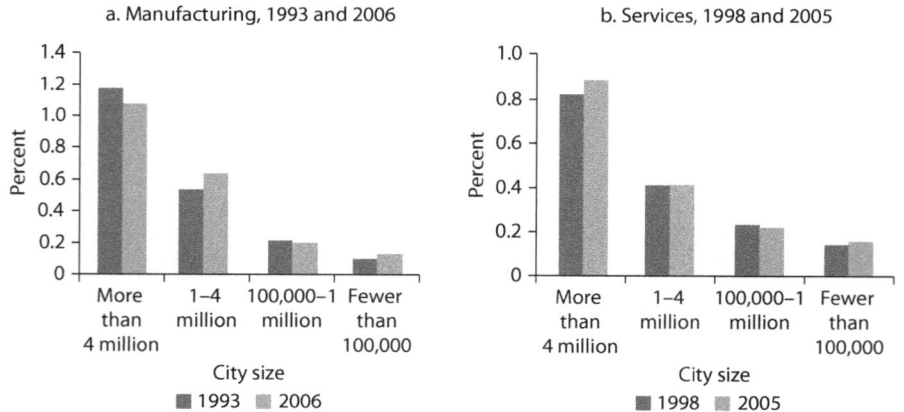

a. Manufacturing, 1993 and 2006

b. Services, 1998 and 2005

1993   2006

1998   2005

Sources: Manufacturing trends are based on Ministry of Statistics and Programme Implementation (1993 and 2006). Services trends are based on Ministry of Statistics and Programme Implementation (1998 and 2005).
Note: The figures show the average district share in national employment in each district group.

was stagnant, even falling in the big seven metropolitan cores and their suburban districts, offsetting the gains made by districts in cities with 1–4 million people.[10] Similarly, the right panel shows no more than a hint of rising concentration in services in the two largest categories combined.

How does one interpret this overall stability in spatial patterns of employment? This is a complicated question because development paths differ across countries. Still, international experience suggests that it should be too early for manufacturing concentration in India's leading metropolitan and suburban areas to start leveling off. The aggregate stability in spatial concentration indicates that the forces opposing concentration, such as congestion, are worryingly strong in India's metropolises.

To examine this question further, we take a more granular look at India's metropolitan economies in the next two sections. First, we drill down regionally, looking at North-South differences in economic specialization across metropolitan areas, and second, we look more closely at India's seven largest metropolitan areas.

Take-Off of the South

In many important sectors of the economy, the southern region (Andhra Pradesh, Karnataka, Kerala, and Tamil Nadu) markedly outgrew the northern belt. Employment in the South grew by 39.9 percent between 1998 and 2005, but only 14.6 percent in the North (see table A.12). This disparity was much larger in manufacturing—17.3 percent (1.20 million jobs) in the South versus less than 1.8 percent (0.25 million jobs) in the North. In education, where large regional differences have been studied extensively, the South again outgrew the North—53.7 to 32.6 percent—though the North nearly doubled employment in education within 50 km of the centers of the largest cities. Construction, a nontradable reflection of local economic performance, grew by 39.8 percent in the South and 68.6 percent in the seven largest cities, while contracting by nearly a quarter in the North.

The widening regional disparity is most marked in high-tech manufacturing industries. The South outperformed the North in all manufacturing subcategories analyzed here (fast-growing export, low tech, and high tech). The South enjoyed positive rates of job growth in all manufacturing subcategories, while nationally, manufacturing jobs declined in all subcategories except for low tech. This decline was most striking in high-tech manufacturing, where the North lost nearly a third of all its jobs (figure 2.6). The overall picture is booming manufacturing in the South and rapid manufacturing decline in the North. ICT services jobs, however, are growing very fast across the entire portfolio of settlements.

The geography of job growth is also very different in the North and South. In the South, total job growth was highest within 50 km of the largest cities (55.5 percent) and lowest 50–100 km from such cities (12.3 percent; see table A.12). In the North, exurban (50–100 km from the urban core) growth (17.3 percent) was nearly triple that within 50 km of the largest city centers.

Although there are likely multiple causes for India's North-South divergence, much of the stagnation in the North is explained by the poor performance of the two largest cities of Delhi and Mumbai, and their neighboring areas. Between 1998 and 2005, the national employment shares of Delhi and Mumbai metropolitan areas (within a 50 km radius of the city centers) contracted by 0.5 percentage point and 1.3 percentage points, respectively. However, in Chennai-Hyderabad-Bangalore metropolitan areas (using the same definition), the national employment share rose by 1.1 percentage points. This suggests

Figure 2.6 North-South Differences in Industrial Performance and Spatial Structure, 1998–2005

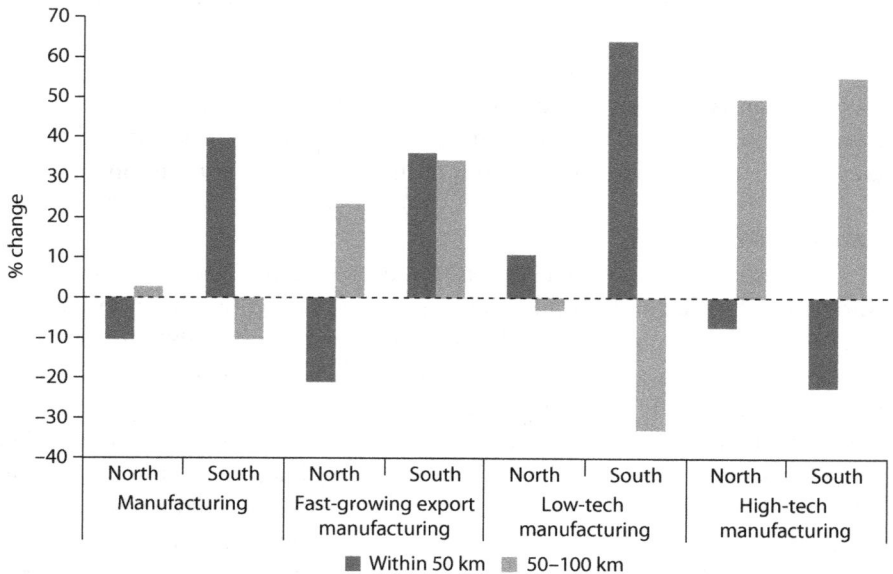

Sources: Ministry of Statistics and Programme Implementation 1998 and 2005.

eroding economic competitiveness of the two largest cities in India. This could be because inflexible metropolitan policies are likely to become binding constraints in the largest metropolises first. This is consistent with the markedly more suburban bent of growth in Delhi and Mumbai than in the Southern cities (see table A.13).

Similar to North versus South, divergence among states in the South is wide, though overall job growth is strong. We focus on Tamil Nadu and Karnataka between 1998 and 2005, specifically the engines of growth, Chennai and Bangalore, and these cities' spatial link with neighboring settlements.

Tamil Nadu's urban job distribution is more balanced than Karnataka's, in that employment in its three largest cities (Chennai, Coimbatore, and Madurai) is 20.0, 5.5, and 4.0 percent of the state total, compared with Karnataka's 27.0, 3.6, and 3.6 percent (Bangalore, Mysore, and Hubli-Dharwad). In Tamil Nadu, Chennai specializes in service activities such as logistics and wholesale and retail trade (39 percent of city jobs), while the next two cities focus on manufacturing (29 and 23 percent of city jobs). The pattern is quite different in Karnataka. Bangalore, Karnataka's largest city, is highly specialized in ICT services (6.3 percent of city jobs, compared with 0.1 and 0.3 percent in the other two cities) and manufacturing (20 percent of city jobs). The second- and third-largest cities of Mysore and Hubli-Dharwad specialize less in manufacturing jobs and more in traded services (see table A.14).

A key contributor to the difference between the two states is likely the favorable geography in Tamil Nadu, namely access to a deep water port. The

Chennai metropolitan area is thriving on jobs linked to trade and logistics. Jobs of fast-growing export manufacturing (in suburban areas in particular), transport, storage, and communications, as well as wholesale and retail trade, are growing much faster in the Chennai metropolitan area, boosted by good connectivity. Related upstream industry jobs, such as construction and real estate as well as low-tech manufacturing (to meet rising local demand) are also growing rapidly around Chennai.

The Bangalore metropolitan area shows a different development path. About 340 km or five hours from Chennai, the Bangalore area is developing footloose or high-tech industries, such as ICT services, which do not require large transport volumes (relative to product value). Nationally, the number of ICT services jobs within 25 km of the city center of the seven largest cities is about 60 times higher than in the next ring (25–50 km). In Bangalore, the ratio is about 1,350—an absolute concentration of ICT jobs in India's Silicon Valley. The massive ICT industrial base in Bangalore is also incubating high-tech manufacturing jobs locally. Similarly, the city's ability to specialize in ICT stems from early investments in education, which nurtured a base of skilled workers (box 2.4). Compared with Chennai, the Bangalore metropolitan area has managed to attract a larger volume of medium- and high-tech manufacturing jobs.

Box 2.4 Bangalore Has Nurtured Skills Beautifully but Must Now Tackle Infrastructure

An analysis of the factors that have contributed to Bangalore's success shows that in 1998 the city's incomes were 24 percent higher than the national average, but nearly 70 percent higher in 2005—a surge of 73 percent.

The skills of the city's residents are the bedrock of its economic success. These skills have early origins, with the Maharajas of the princely state of Mysore instituting compulsory education, building the University of Mysore and Bangalore's engineering college. This was the starting point for the cluster of educated engineers that persists to this day. Building on an initial corpus of engineering expertise, firms such as Infosys were attracted to Bangalore, jump-starting a virtuous circle where smart companies and smart workers come to a city to be close to one another.

However, Bangalore's economic success is creating its own infrastructure problems, including poor water quality, traffic congestion, and housing shortages. The water system is strained: 30 percent of city residents use polluted groundwater, the sewer system does not reach a large part of the city, and average commute times are more than 40 minutes because jobs are dispersed from the city core. If the water problems or commuting times get worse, skilled people—the city's main asset—will leave for cities that offer better amenities. How Bangalore improves the quality of life for its residents will have a considerable bearing on how bright Bangalore continues to shine.

Source: Glaeser 2010.

In sum, even though Chennai and Bangalore are in neighboring states, their local economic structure is quite different, with economic geography undoubtedly playing a large role. Further analysis is necessary to fully identify the relative importance of localization (Chennai) versus urbanization (Bangalore) economies in Indian cities in general, as well as these two, and to establish causal relationships among policy interventions, economic geography conditions, and specialization patterns.

Metropolitan Suburbanization

A rapid spatial restructuring lies behind the seemingly stable economic concentration in India's largest metropolitan areas, according to spatially detailed data from the 1998 and 2005 economic censuses.[11] The suburbs and peripheries are gaining industry, while metropolitan cores are deindustrializing (see figure 2.7).

The largest seven metropolitan cores (defined as areas within 10 km of the city center) are losing manufacturing employment (figure 2.7): it fell by 16 percent between 1998 and 2005. Yet in the suburbs and immediate peripheries (a 50 km radius excluding the core), it rose by nearly 12 percent, a rate twice the national average. This readjustment between the cores and suburbs is most evident in high-tech and fast-growing export manufacturing industries: the cores saw a 60 percent drop in high-tech industries, while the suburbs saw a 60 percent rise in that segment.

Figure 2.7 Employment Growth in Metropolitan Cores and Peripheries by Sector, 1998–2005

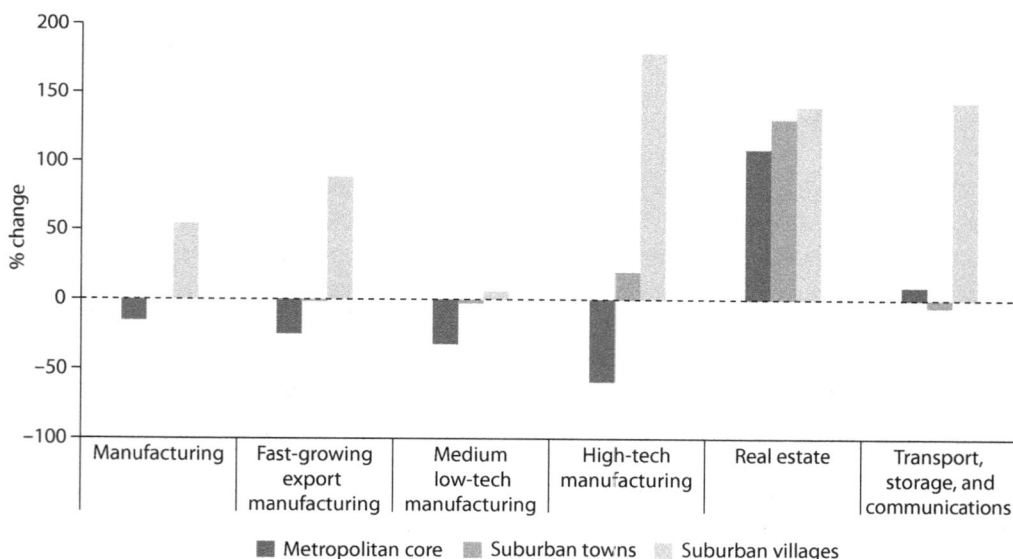

■ Metropolitan core   ■ Suburban towns   ■ Suburban villages

Sources: Ministry of Statistics and Programme Implementation 1998 and 2005.
Note: Metropolitan core includes an area with a radius of 10 km centered on the main metropolis. Suburban towns include urban areas 10 to 50 km from the metropolitan core, and suburban villages include rural areas in the same vicinity. These figures are averages for the seven largest metropolitan areas (in descending order of population): Mumbai, Delhi, Bangalore, Kolkata, Chennai, Hyderabad, and Ahmedabad.

All suburban areas (between 10 and 50 km from the urban core)—whether officially classified as rural or urban—are experiencing the same manufacturing boom. In fact, at 54 percent, the pace of manufacturing employment growth was fastest in rural areas adjacent to the largest metropolitan areas over 1998–2005. While we observe overall stagnancy of the big seven metropolitan areas, there is clear evidence that high-tech and other emerging manufacturing industries are relocating to the immediate suburbs and peripheries of these very cities, not to locations farther away. Moreover, though metropolitan suburbanization is a worldwide phenomenon, it usually happens at middle to advanced stages of development.[12] Thus India's early suburbanization suggests that the overall stagnancy of metropolitan areas is partly due to firms being pushed out of the cores. The next section offers an overview of why, which chapter 3 takes up in more detail.

Policy Distortions Hindering Economic and Spatial Transformation
The diagnostics of India's urbanization highlights considerable stability in the spatial distribution of people and jobs. One would have expected rapid economic concentration in large metropolitan areas with good market access following India's economic liberalization. This is what was seen after China's economic liberalization in the 1980s and in dynamic emerging economies that rapidly urbanized and industrialized. But India's metropolitan areas have not experienced discernible gains in economic activity. This stagnancy points toward three overlapping scenarios.

First, industry overall in India has not grown rapidly, thus reducing the demand for urban agglomerations that can generate localization and urbanization economies. However, this argument is not entirely convincing as India has developed niche markets in ICT services and specialized manufacturing that it trades with the rest of the world. Also there has been considerable growth in low-end manufacturing consumed and traded domestically. And by looking at differences among urban areas in India's fast-growing South and stagnating North—it is becoming clear that economic geography has a role to play in influencing relative economic specialization across urban areas.

Second, Indian cities have restrictive rules on conversion of land for urban uses, and the intensity at which land can be used by industry, commerce, and housing. For example, even though the international best practice in cities with limited land (as in Singapore and Hong Kong SAR, China) is to raise the permitted floor space index (FSI)—the ratio of the gross floor area of a building on a lot divided by the area of that lot—to accommodate growth, the Municipal Corporation of Greater Mumbai went the other way, lowering the permitted FSI to 1.33 in 1991 (World Bank 2008). In India's otherwise liberalized policy environment, stringent regulations on development densities are pushing businesses and people out of urban cores. These constraints on land use are also making housing expensive, pricing out poor and middle-class households from urban centers.

Third, the growth of metropolitan suburbs may well be a reaction to draconian land policy. However, the journey to the suburbs is costly for firms and workers.

Transport costs for freight are among the highest nationally between the metropolitan core and its periphery, and infrastructure access and quality for water, electricity, and sanitation is much worse in the urban periphery than in the core.

Next, chapter 3 examines specificities of policy distortions in land and infrastructure and the constraints that hold back provision of infrastructure and housing.

Notes

1. A good discussion of the index is provided in Uchida and Nelson (2008).

2. For example, Sriperambudur near Chennai, Noida and Gurgaon near Delhi, and Raigarh near Mumbai.

3. In descending order: Mumbai, Delhi, Bangalore, Kolkata, Chennai, Hyderabad, and Ahmedabad.

4. India estimates from a specially commissioned transport survey (see next chapter), and China estimates from Bansal (2005).

5. Medium high-tech industries include inorganic chemicals, precious metal compounds, and isotopes; organic chemicals; photographic or cinematographic goods; miscellaneous chemical products; rubber and articles; articles of iron or steel; machinery, nuclear reactors, boilers, and the like; electrical and electronic equipment; railway, tramway locomotives, rolling stock, and equipment; vehicles other than railway and tramway; optical, photo, technical, and medical apparatus; clocks, watches, and parts; and musical instruments, parts, and accessories. High-tech industries are pharmaceutical products and aircraft, spacecraft, and parts.

6. Fast-growing export manufacturing industries are electrical and electronic equipment; machinery, nuclear reactors, boilers, and the like; organic chemicals; vehicles other than railway and tramway; articles of apparel: knit or crochet; accessories and pharmaceutical products; iron, steel, and articles of iron or steel; and ships, boats, and other floating structures. The selection is based on export growth between 2009 and 2011. ICT services are those listed under 72 (two-digit code) of the 2004 National Industry Classification (computer and related activities).

7. An administrative subdivision or tier of local government of some 100–350 villages.

8. Ministry of Statistics and Programme Implementation 2005.

9. A threshold of 1 means that local representation is the same as national representation—parity.

10. District data on all manufacturing employment (including establishments smaller than factories) from the economic censuses of 1998 and 2005 show the same trends (Ministry of Statistics and Programme Implementation 1998 and 2005).

11. Ministry of Statistics and Programme Implementation 1998 and 2005.

12. See Townroe (1981) and Hansen (1983) for Brazil, and Chun and Lee (1985) and Henderson, Lee, and Lee (1999) for Korea. One review paper highlighted that the general trend of urban development included dispersal from the center to the periphery of both population and employment, with the largest metropolitan areas converging to decentralized and multiple subcentered areas (Ingram 1998).

References

Bairoch, Paul. 1988. *Cities and Economic Development: From the Dawn of History to the Present.* Chicago: University of Chicago Press.

Bansal, Alok. 2005. "Issues in Freight Transport—India." World Bank, Washington, DC.

Chun, Dong Hoon, and Kyu Sik Lee. 1985. "Changing Location Patterns of Population and Employment in the Seoul Region." Discussion paper UDD65, World Bank, Washington, DC.

Glaeser, Edward L. 2010. *Making Sense of Bangalore.* London: Legatum Institute.

Hansen, Eric R. 1983. "Why Do Firms Locate Where They Do?" Discussion paper UDD25, World Bank, Washington, DC.

Henderson, J. Vernon, T. Lee, and J-Y Lee. 1999. "Externalities and Industrial Deconcentration under Rapid Growth." Brown University, Providence, RI.

Ingram, Gregory K. 1998. "Patterns of Metropolitan Development: What Have We Learned?" *Urban Studies* 35 (7): 1019–35.

Ministry of Home Affairs. 2001. "Census of India: Census Data 2001." Office of the Registrar General and Census Commissioner, New Delhi.

Ministry of Statistics and Programme Implementation. 1993. "Annual Survey of Industries." New Delhi.

———. 1994. "Annual Survey of Industries 1993–94." New Delhi.

———. 1998. "Economic Census 1998: All India Report." Central Statistical Organisation, New Delhi.

———. 2005. "Provisional Results of Economic Census 2005: All India Report." Central Statistical Organisation, New Delhi.

———. 2006. "Annual Survey of Industries." New Delhi.

———. 2007. "Annual Survey of Industries 2006." New Delhi.

Schneider, Annemarie, Mark A. Friedl, and David Potere. 2009. "A New Map of Global Urban Extent from MODIS Data." *Environmental Research Letters* 4 (4): Article 044003.

Townroe, Peter. 1981. "Location Factors in the Decentralization of Industry: A Survey of Metropolitan São Paulo." Staff working paper 517, World Bank, Washington, DC.

Uchida, Hirotsugu, and Andrew Nelson. 2008. "Agglomeration Index: Towards a New Measure of Urban Concentration." Background Paper for the *World Development Report 2009.* World Bank, Washington, DC.

World Bank. 2008. *World Development Report 2009: Reshaping Economic Geography.* Washington, DC: World Bank.

———. 2011. *Urbanization Review—South Korea.* Washington, DC: Korea Research Institute for Human Settlements.

CHAPTER 3

Policy Distortions and Infrastructure Bottlenecks

Introduction

Suburbanization patterns in India are consistent with international experience, though occurring at a far lower per capita GDP. This early onset may be because India's suburban areas suffer from regulatory constraints and infrastructure short-falls, such that overall metropolitan stagnation and the concomitant growth of economic activity and people on the outskirts of India's largest cities may reflect a push out of the metropolitan cores. India's suburbanization—especially in manufacturing, where scale economies and access to land are important—suggests that inflexible land and related infrastructure policies are reducing the pull of metropolitan economies.

This chapter delves more deeply into the challenges Indian cities face in accommodating urban expansion, which include a lack of independent valuation systems; stringent urban planning rules; little coordination between planned changes to land use and proposed infrastructure improvements; expensive housing; long commuting times, as well as steep commuting and freight costs; and variable and often unreliable access to basic services.

Much of the analysis is descriptive and does not address issues of causality, but rather it points to specific distortions that may be preventing India from reaping the full benefits of urbanization.

Pace and Shape of Urban Expansion Distorted by Rigid Land Policies

Urbanization brings with it an increase in the demand for land, and a problem arises when land is scarce in places it is needed the most. The initial focus in this chapter on land stems from the need to identify options for land transactions to accommodate urban expansion as cities extend beyond their administrative boundaries. The rules that impede land use transformation from rural to urban uses will in turn have effects on housing supply, connectivity, and basic infra-structure provision, topics discussed later in this chapter.

Land acquisition is part of the strategy employed by many countries—including India—to make land available for urban and infrastructure development. In fact, land acquisition policies are at the center of the policy debate on urbanization in India. The draft Land Acquisition and Rehabilitation and Resettlement (LARR) bill attempts to balance efficiency from urbanization and infrastructure development with equity for displaced residents (box 3.1).

Beyond land acquisition, the repurposing of existing urban areas to new demands is needed. Yet urban planning systems in India make it harder to expand, redevelop, or modernize older, inefficient urban areas. Urban plans seek to preserve current land use by limiting land assembly and freezing the density of development by using very low floor space indexes (FSIs).

Box 3.1   India Acknowledges the Need for Land Policy Reform

India lacks many of the institutions required for well-functioning land markets. For example, the process of public land acquisition using the power of eminent domain (compulsory purchase) under the current law, which dates from 1894, has often been nontransparent, with significant opportunities for corruption.

India lacks a transparent system to convert land use, a clear definition of property rights, a robust system of land and property valuation, and a strong judicial system for addressing public concerns to facilitate land-market functioning. The draft Land Acquisition and Rehabilitation and Resettlement (LARR) bill acknowledges the need for land policy reform but does not solve the complex issue of unclear property rights. There are also problems in the way the bill's compensation is assigned. While it puts forward a suggested method for valuing land in this context, it does not fully address the core issues of land valuation in India. There are also problems with the bill's proposed compensation system, for two main reasons.

First, India does not have a system to provide independent and reliable valuations of land. Onerous stamp duties, which the LARR bill refers to, have historically created incentives to underreport land and property values—and surveys infrequently update these values. Thus, institutions should be built that improve the information foundations of the valuation process, which would include training a cadre of appraisers in property valuation, ensuring transparency and consistency in valuation (to get public acceptance), and making information of land values widely accessible (to deter corruption). Without the institutional capacity to help discover and disseminate the value of land, the acquisition process offers considerable scope for undervaluing it. But this cannot be achieved unless stamp duties are reduced from their extremely high rates.

Second, laws in many countries provide for valuation by independent persons or bodies, rather than by the acquiring authorities. Thus, although the draft bill provides ample opportunity for contesting valuation decisions, greater independence of the valuation expertise along with engagement of affected persons in valuation discussions early in the process could be considered.

Source: Urbanization Review team.

A framework for sequencing and implementing land policy reform is needed, to allow policy makers to consider options for accommodating and financing India's urban expansion. At early stages of urbanization, policies that facilitate rural–urban land use conversion will be critical to support urban expansion. Creating strong institutions that facilitate this transformation and help reduce transaction costs as well as information asymmetries will contribute to enhancing the fluidity of nascent land markets. Clear definition of property rights and valuation can set the foundations for well-functioning land markets proposed reforms through the LARR bill that is being debated by government and civil society.

Nascent Valuation Systems

The success of tools used for accommodating urban expansion is typically based on robust systems for determining land values. Developed countries rely on various forms of data and institutions to assess land values, including market data on transactions and attributes of the property, as well as ancillary data on potential income from land and the cost of inputs into land development. These data are managed to provide up-to-date and reliable information for professional appraisers and the general public.

Institutions that improve the information foundations of the valuation process, including a trained cadre of appraisers in property valuation, contribute to ensuring transparency in the valuation process and to making information on land values widely accessible. In the Republic of Korea until the early 1970s, local government officials assessed the market value and replacement costs of assets for land-acquisition purposes. In 1972, the government introduced the Basic Land Prices system, to improve assessments. In this new system, land and buildings had to be assessed by certified private appraisers rather than government officials. Two such appraisers had to provide estimated values for the property and the final value was obtained as the average of the two values. If the two appraisals differed by more than 10 percent, a third appraiser was selected and the average recalculated. Since 2003, a third appraiser may be recommended by affected individuals as well (ADB 2007).

Developing countries often lack the systems to record and manage information on land transactions. The data may not, for instance, reflect the true price of land because of black market transactions to save on duties or heavy public subsidies on housing and land use. Land registries are often archaic and lack the dynamic functions that allow them to be searched or updated quickly.

These deficiencies translate into a dearth of data on real estate prices, preventing analysis that is critical for appraising land values, with heavy implications for real estate–based local financing. Land valuation is integral to local revenue generation since land values form the basis for activities such as property tax collection and land sales or leases.

In India, such information systems are in their infancy and rely on assessments based on stamp duties to reveal the price of land.[1] However, these stamp values are usually lower bound estimates of market values because India's historically high stamp duties created incentives to underreport land and property values, which surveys too rarely update.

In countries where land valuation is successful, techniques are standardized to enable appraisers to arrive at uniform and transparent valuations. In the United States, most states require that appraisers and assessors be certified. Appraisers generally work for private clients to determine the market value of property for real estate transactions, while assessors generally work for the government to determine values of properties for tax purposes (United States Department of Labor 2010). Both must follow the same regulations in valuing real estate. However, for practical purposes and to avoid overestimation of prices, property prices for tax purposes are often set at about two-thirds of actual market value. In Bogotá, property values are usually set at 70–80 percent of estimated market value.

Public land valuation in developing countries is fraught with challenges, including the cost of hiring private assessors (as these countries lack standardized public valuation methods), the need to update land price data, and the fact that intergovernment transfers of public land are often recorded as a zero value transaction. They can be overcome, however, as seen in at least two cases of innovation in public land valuation. Kuwait now requires two separate private appraisals for public-private partnerships (Peterson and Kaganova 2010). And South Africa mandates that public land be taxed the same way as private land, which means that public land undergoes the same valuation processes (Peterson and Kaganova 2010). Yet many other developing countries still struggle to value public land, and auctions are often used to reveal land values.

In Germany, federal regulation governs private land valuation.[2] Germany has local land valuation boards that are charged with collecting and maintaining land price data as well as disseminating land price information (Kertscher 2004; Seidel 2006).

The United States allows each state to define its own method for private property valuation. In most cases, states delegate this power to local governments, leading to a vast array of approaches. While the most common is the market value (or sales comparison) approach, there are at least two others: the cost approach, and the income approach.[3] All three approaches are often used in parallel to estimate property values. New York, for example, uses these methods for different property categories. It follows the sales comparison approach to value small residential properties and vacant land, using sales data of comparable properties for the previous three years. It adopts the income approach to value offices and businesses, taking an estimated income and dividing the net income by a capitalization rate. It uses the cost approach for new construction and renovations and for special properties such as stadiums, museums, and places of worship (Lafuente 2009).

Over the longer term, it is important for India to build the necessary institutions for land valuation, but it should explore alternatives as intermediate solutions for the short and medium term. Indeed, recent work by Ghatak and Ghosh (2011) for India proposes an auction system for land valuation where displaced farmers are given the option to choose between compensation in land or cash, while the area of intervention is extended to include farmland surrounding the project area. Further, the government could explore methods of assembling land for infrastructure in a participatory environment, such as land readjustment. These methods are discussed in detail in chapter 4.

Sprawl and Property Price Effects of Stringent Land Regulations

Just as valuing land and assigning property rights are challenges for accommodating urban expansion, so is managing densities within cities and finding ways to finance urban expansion and city renewal. One widely used tool for managing densities is the FSI.[4] This is the ratio of the gross floor area of a building on a lot divided by the area of that lot. So, for example, if the FSI in an area of a city is 1:1, developers can only put up a building with a gross floor area less than or equal to the total lot area. While in some cases it may be possible to build a one-story building that covers the lot entirely, thus achieving an FSI of 1:1, developers typically construct buildings with a "footprint" or "plinth" that covers less than the whole lot and build a more than one-story structure. For example, a developer could cover 25 percent of the lot and build a four-story building and still meet the FSI of 1:1.

Planning regulations also set maximum building heights and standards for how close buildings can be from the front, rear, and sides of the lot, known as setback requirements. These ensure that adjacent properties are not adversely affected by new development and that existing users have access to sun, ventilation, and in some cases open spaces (plazas, pocket parks, and so on). They also use lot-coverage ratio regulations to limit the total area of a lot that can be developed.

Because economic transformation is changing land use demands, cities need to reorient their built environment. However, highly restrictive urban planning controls—FSI regulations, height, lot size, setback, and zoning controls—may impose limits on development. Map 3.1 shows FSI regulations in Mumbai, which have two striking features.

First, Mumbai's FSI ratios, at around 1.0–1.5—low compared with international standards (discussed further below)—have significant consequences. Low FSIs generate sprawl as development is forced to the periphery of the urban area. Sprawl is due to limits on real estate development in areas where the market would otherwise call for higher density to compensate for high land prices resulting from high accessibility. FSI-induced sprawl has costs—for example, causing welfare losses in Bangalore of 1.5–4.5 percent of household income owing to higher commuting costs (box 3.2).

Second, Mumbai's FSI regulations do not exhibit the fine granular patterns seen in cities like New York, Seoul, and Singapore, but are the same across large areas of the city, failing to reflect variations in infrastructure capacity and accessibility.

Mumbai and Bangalore are examples of a broader practice among Indian urban planners, who argue that densities need to be kept low to avoid

Map 3.1 Maximum FSIs in Mumbai

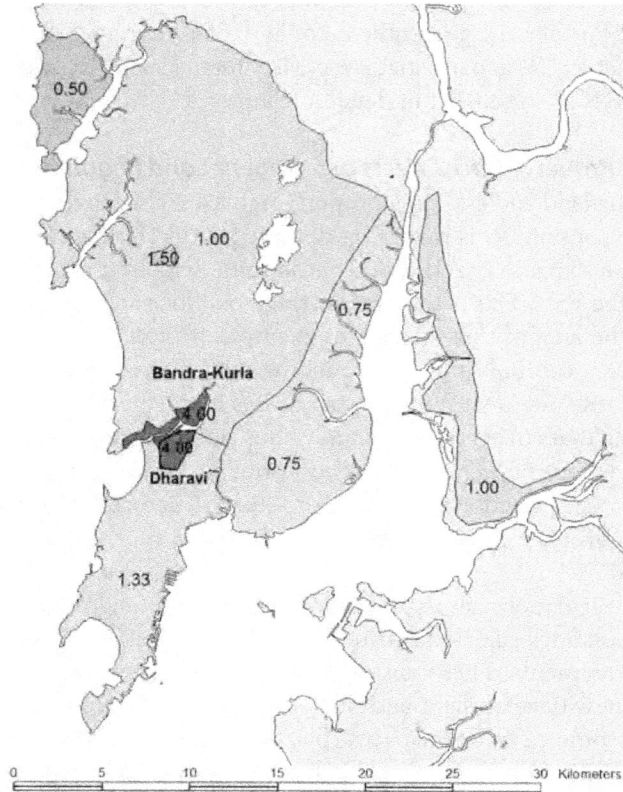

Source: © Alain Bertaud. Reproduced with permission from Bertaud (2004); further permission required for reuse.
Note: FSI = floor space index.

a breakdown in existing infrastructure systems of most cities. This very lack of infrastructure is the principal argument that planners use to justify keeping FSIs low. They argue that existing urban areas should be preserved and development shifted to new towns and suburban industrial estates. However, although Indian cities have severe infrastructure limits, these arguments ignore the opportunities of using gains in land values to finance higher capacity and higher quality infrastructure and to increase the supply of office space and affordable housing for low- and middle-income groups. They also ignore that if urban planning permitted more compact development, cities' economic density would increase, stimulating gains in agglomeration economies and in productivity.

Keeping FSIs low suppresses economic growth, most importantly exacerbating housing shortages and affordability (see box 3.2). Cities' plans and zoning designations need to reflect market realities. If a city does not zone enough land for a particular use, the supply of land for that use will be constrained, causing land prices to rise. It is thus important that the master plan (including zoning designations) be based on market demand and that land use and densities reflect

---

Box 3.2 Building-Height Restrictions Induce Spatial Expansion

Bertaud and Brueckner (2004) estimate the economic costs of building-height restrictions on Bangalore, using a model that makes it possible to estimate the effects of restrictions on a city's physical size.

They find that removing FSI restrictions—binding up to the first 5 kilometers (km) from the center and covering 24 percent of the city's built-up area—would have led to a city with a 10 percent smaller built-up area. It would also have shrunk the periphery from 12 to 8 km from the city center (figure B3.2.1).

The resulting shorter commuting distances would have saved 1.5–4.5 percent of household income, excluding any productivity improvements from shorter commutes or other gains from higher agglomeration in the city center.

Figure B3.2.1 Effects of Removing FSI Restrictions

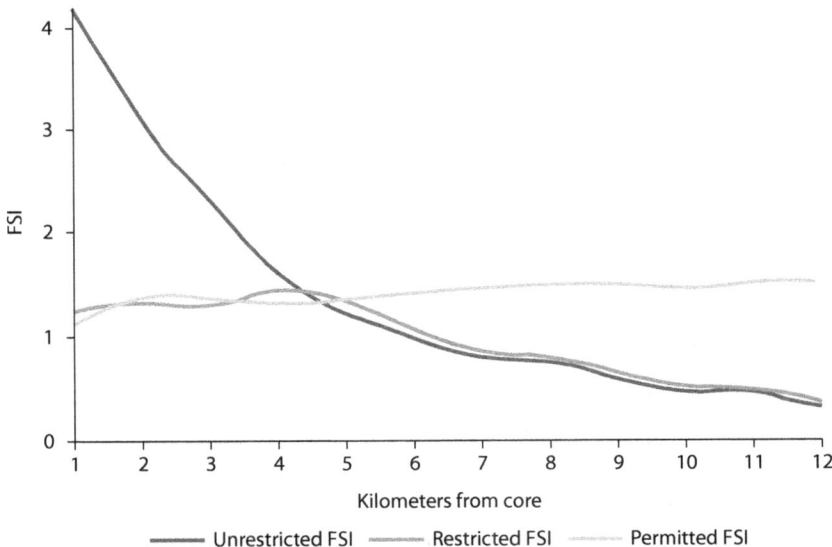

Source: Bertaud and Brueckner 2004.
Note: FSI = floor space index.

---

market realities. The consequence of master plans that artificially limit land supply can be soaring land prices. When plans underestimate required land uses, such as residential, industrial, commercial, and services, land prices for parcels zoned as such tend to sell at higher prices than would be set in the marketplace. This stems directly from the creation of "scarcity rents."

Experience in other countries indicates that India may benefit from an urban planning paradigm shift—plans need to be strategic, flexible, accommodative, and continuous. This means that master plans and zoning regulations for residential use need to reflect anticipated demand from migration, new household formation, and demand for more space as incomes rise. The same dynamic applies to nonresidential uses: if industrial, commercial, or services uses are overly limited, land prices in these categories will rise above market-clearing prices, leading to high occupancy (box 3.3).

An FSI set significantly below its market equilibrium has negative consequences, imposing heavy costs on the city's economy. For example, it increases the demand for land across the city because more land is required for the same amount of floor space, raising land prices (See, for example, Ohls, Weisberg, and White 1974). A uniform restriction on the FSI encourages nonproductive use of housing capital, raises equilibrium housing prices, and lowers city growth.[5]

Further, low FSIs limit the quantity of available formal housing within the city's boundaries, driving up real estate prices and making housing less affordable and commercial space more expensive in constrained areas along with higher prices across the city. Poor households often are pushed to distant suburbs—but these decisions reduce welfare as commuting costs and times are very high.

In less restricted real estate markets, such as Bangkok, private developers have adjusted to the increasing demographic and economic pressures as well as to rising land and construction prices. They raised the density of housing projects during 1974–88—a period of rapid urban growth and rising land and housing construction prices. The average number of units per hectare rose from 35 to 56, and multifamily housing units rose from less than 2 percent of the new construction in 1986 to 43 percent in 1990 (Dowall 1992). Such shifts allowed developers to continue to provide affordable housing and still earn a profit.

Box 3.3 A Greenbelt around Seoul Imposed Heavy Restrictions on Land Supply and Led to Steep Increases in Land Prices

In Seoul, the Korean government established a greenbelt ordinance in 1971 that rigorously restricted urbanization in greenbelt areas. The greenbelt did not initially affect land and real estate prices because the area inside the belt where urban growth was permitted was enough to accommodate new urban development: in 1972, that area was 554 square kilometers, against a total urbanized area of less than half that (206 square kilometers).

But by 1989 all the area inside the belt was urbanized, land prices started to escalate, and housing became less affordable. Real land prices that year were three times as high as in 1970. The house-price to household-income ratio increased to 9.3, the fifth highest in the world.[a]

Seoul's greenbelt policies have caused the supply of urban housing to be highly inelastic, and thus drive up land and housing prices, as demand increased over time.[b] Knapp (1985) examined the effects of Portland's Urban Growth Boundary on land prices and concluded that after controlling for distance to the center of Portland, Oregon, prices inside the boundary were higher than those outside.

a. Lee 1999.
b. Cho 1992; Green, Malpezzi, and Vandell 1994; Hannah, Kim, and Mills 1993; Kim 1987.

In 1986–90, almost half the increase in Bangkok's housing stock was produced by private developers, while informally produced housing constituted a mere 3 percent of the total. In contrast, informally produced housing in cities with highly constrained land markets constituted 20–80 percent of the total (Dowall 1998).

When FSIs are not granular, cities lose opportunities for increasing density in areas with wide streets and suitable infrastructure capacity. Worse, geographically expansive, low FSIs freeze new development and modernization. Because of low FSIs, developers may be unable to substitute capital for land to overcome high land prices (figure 3.1).

Another adverse impact of a very low FSI is that it distorts the spatial structure of cities. In Mumbai, the historical central business district (near Churchgate station) is at the southern tip of the peninsula when in fact the Bandra Kurla center would be a more centralized and more accessible location for dense business and financial services. While the FSI in the Bandra Kurla area is 1:4, it is still very low by international standards—FSIs in central business districts in best practice cities (New York, Seoul, and Singapore) exceed 1:10. The result of a low FSI in Bandra Kurla is that it may not develop as intensively as it should and will thus have difficulties attracting businesses and commercial activities at a scale necessary to form a "second central business district."

In sum, FSI restrictions drive up real estate prices in areas where the regulations limit development below what an unregulated market would generate. They are also likely to drive up land prices on the periphery of cities as

Figure 3.1 Hypothetical Example of the Effect of FSI Regulations on Building Density

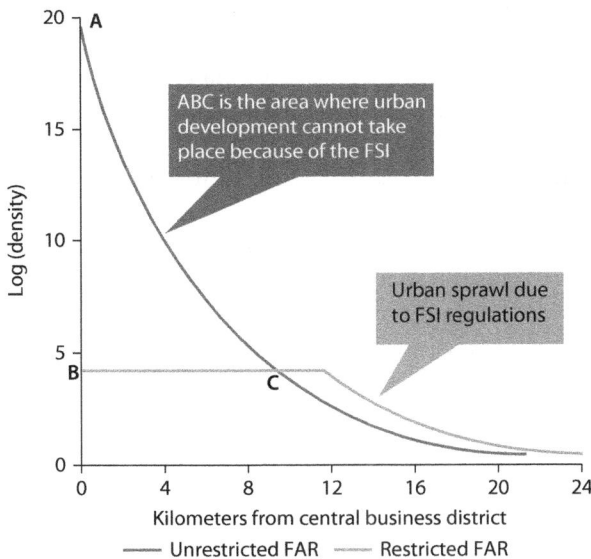

Source: Bertaud and Brueckner 2004.
Note: FAR = floor area ratio; FSI = floor space index.

development is pushed out of the central area into suburban areas. These price increases reduce housing affordability and cause businesses to consider other suburban locations, cities, or countries. Finally, because households are forced to either underconsume housing or locate in the suburbs because of higher housing prices, they suffer a welfare loss in commuting due to the FSIs. With urban living standards lower, cities look less attractive to potential migrants, and the upshot may be slower urbanization than in a less regulated setting. Barriers that otherwise impede development (such as inadequate methods of land valuation) can also contribute to this urbanization slowdown.

Little Land Use and Infrastructure Coordination

Despite the focus on FSIs in the previous section, they are part of an overall planning strategy and cannot be considered in isolation.[6] Beyond that, decisions on FSIs and infrastructure investment should be taken jointly, achieving a virtuous circle. If FSIs increase to allow higher densities, these higher densities should be supported by infrastructure investments. Similarly, places with strong infrastructure can allow higher densities and could thus have higher FSIs.

FSIs provide the opportunity to manage densities by creating mechanisms where initial densities are regulated but developers are allowed to exceed these limits by paying for additional densities. In fact, regulations on coverage areas and FSIs can be combined to create different density structures. Yet there is no optimal FSI. The level of the FSI depends on many things—existing spatial structure, street patterns, infrastructure capacity, and social and cultural factors. The key lesson: FSIs and these elements must be linked to formulate efficient and desirable spatial structures. For large metropolitan areas, this typically means moving from a monocentric spatial structure with only one central business district to a polycentric structure with multiple, well-connected activity centers.

The range of FSIs can be considerable, running from 1:1 to 1:25 (table 3.1). Except for São Paulo (where the FSI is much lower than in the city's central business district), most of the lowest FSIs are in India. Other cities have much higher FSIs—ranging from 1:3 for Paris to 1:25 for Singapore. Most of the cities with high FSIs have high rates of infrastructure services per hectare.

Most FSI maps for best practice cities, such as New York, Seoul, and Singapore (see maps 3.2, 3.3 below) show a fine-grain pattern of small density zones, determined by street width and capacity, existing land use patterns,[7] and infrastructure capacity. Areas of cities that are economically dynamic, such as central business districts, generally have the highest FSIs. These areas are well served by transit systems and can accommodate large daytime populations. Outlying areas adjacent to transit stations or where highways intersect also have higher FSIs, because planners view this as a useful strategy to increase uptake of the transit system and limit car use.

FSIs in New York's Manhattan borough vary by location and by land use. Commercial activities in midtown and downtown are much higher than in residential areas on the upper east and west sides (map 3.2).

Table 3.1 Variation of FSIs in Central Business Districts

City	Central business district FSI
São Paulo, Brazil	1:1[a]
Mumbai, India	1:1.33
Chennai, India	1:1.5
Delhi, India	1:1.2–1:3.5
Amsterdam, Netherlands	1:1.9
Venice, Italy	1:2.4
Paris, France	1:3
Shanghai, China	1:8
Vancouver, Canada	1:8
San Francisco, United States	1:9
Chicago, United States	1:12
Hong Kong SAR, China	1:12
Los Angeles, United States	1:13
New York, United States	1:15
Denver, United States	1:17
Tokyo, Japan	1:20
Singapore	1:12–1:25

Source: Lainton 2011.
Note: FSI = floor space index.
a. The central business district FSI uses transfers of development rights.

Seoul also has used FSIs to increase development potential and density inside the greenbelt (map 3.3). The increases in FSI and density have sparked a sharp increase in redevelopment and revitalization in the city. In Seoul, as in New York and Singapore, city planners have been very selective in designating FSI levels so that they are closely aligned with infrastructure (mainly transit capacity) but also water and sanitation, pedestrian flows, and policies to develop commercial and mixed commercial and residential activity centers. This alignment of FSIs with infrastructure capacity leads to a granular approach to setting FSIs. All three cities have designed their master plan, zoning, and FSI regulations to conform with plan projections of population and employment growth. The regulations manage and guide development and minimize negative externalities but do not overly constrain urban development.

To effectively shape the spatial structure, density, and land use pattern of a city or metropolitan area, planners work with the master plans to prepare more detailed district plans, draft zoning ordinances to implement the plan, and pre-pare FSI regulations to limit building density. Even before they go into detail, planners need to set FSI regulations when they formulate infrastructure plans. Density should not overwhelm infrastructure capacity—nor should it constrain the optimal use of infrastructure networks by keeping density below what the infrastructure can support. Optimizing infrastructure and density is thus a cen-tral element of urban planning.

Beyond regulations, most city and metropolitan plans provide incentives to encourage developers to build projects consistent with existing master plans.

Map 3.2 Manhattan's Granular Density Assignments to Leverage Infrastructure Capacity

FSI variations in Manhattan's zoning

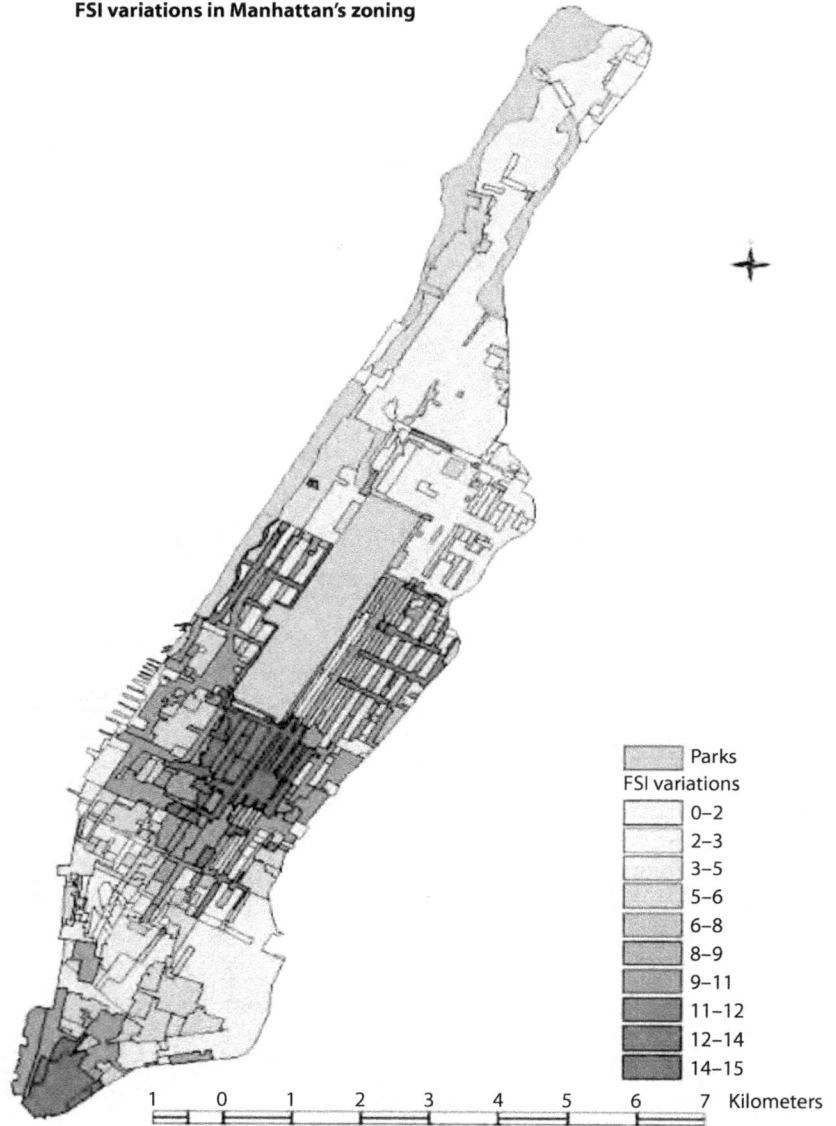

Parks
FSI variations
- 0–2
- 2–3
- 3–5
- 5–6
- 6–8
- 8–9
- 9–11
- 11–12
- 12–14
- 14–15

1   0   1   2   3   4   5   6   7 Kilometers

Source: © New York City Planning Department. Reproduced with permission from New York City Planning Department (2011); further permission required for reuse.
Note: In some zones, the floor space index (FSI) might be increased up to two additional units because of bonuses due to plaza, arcades, and the like. In some areas, the permitted FSI might not be reached because of setbacks and plot geometry.

The most common instruments are public provision of infrastructure services, density bonuses and controls, and transferable development rights (TDRs).

Cities' provision of new infrastructure services in areas with deficiencies is highly effective in promoting desired development and spatial structure. Buenos Aires, Cape Town, and Sydney, for example, have refurbished their historical port

Map 3.3 FSI Variations Linked to Infrastructure Corridors, Seoul

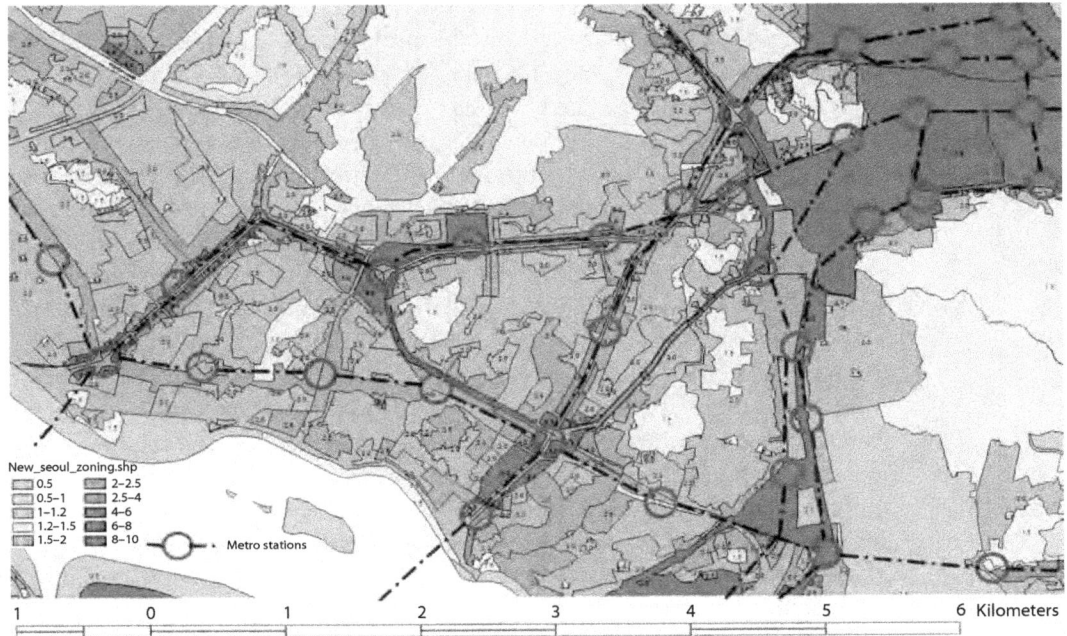

New_seoul_zoning.shp
- 0.5
- 0.5–1
- 1–1.2
- 1.2–1.5
- 1.5–2
- 2–2.5
- 2.5–4
- 4–6
- 6–8
- 8–10
- Metro stations

1   0   1   2   3   4   5   6 Kilometers

Source: © Alain Bertaud. Reproduced with permission from Bertaud (2008); further permission required for reuse.

and maritime districts and enhanced infrastructure, turning these areas into major activity centers. One important aspect of using infrastructure investment to promote denser development is to consider using value capture tools to garner some of the land value increases generated by the investment. Many cities charge developers development impact fees to recoup some of the land value gain and use it to partly finance the infrastructure investments (Fulton and Shigley 2005). In other cities, governments have offered density bonuses to developers that build apartments and office buildings around new or existing transit stations, a practice used in China, the United States, and Europe.[8]

The TDR is a special type of density bonus (Costonis 1974). In many cities, planners allow developers to purchase "extra" development rights (enabling them to build at higher densities) from property owners unwilling or uninterested in using their full development rights (typically, not wanting to demolish structures and redevelop). Instead, they sell some of their rights to other property owners or developers so that they can build at a higher than permitted density. These development transfers are generally used to encourage preservation of historic buildings by allowing existing owners the possibility of gaining compensation for maintaining low-rise, low-density buildings. One way to value TDRs is to create a market for the exchange of floor space rights and let demand and supply set prices—the process used in New York and São Paulo, for example.

Both FSI bonuses and TDR incentives can be highly effective, but they need to be closely aligned with the infrastructure capacity of the area "receiving" them.

If the additional density conferred on an area overwhelms current infrastructure, large problems can quickly develop. A few years ago, Panama City granted TDRs to condominium developers, but as the projects started filling up, they overwhelmed the city's sewerage network and raw sewage flooded several new projects, underscoring the need for such alignment (BBC 2011).

In Mumbai, where FSI in urban areas is very low by international standards, a TDR policy allows denser development in the northern suburbs, but it seems to be causing two problems. First, many of the new, higher density projects have had adverse impacts, such as traffic congestion, as well as less access to sunlight and ventilation. Second, because the transfer zones are outside existing urban areas, they do not create opportunities to develop more modern and compact business and residential districts, particularly in the old central business district or the new Bandra Kurla district.

Because housing conditions in many Indian cities are very poor—slums and overcrowding are common—increases in FSI for residential projects should allow households to purchase or rent larger units, as prices per square meter should fall, implying that doubling the FSI will not automatically double population density, since households will consume more space per capita. Still, as FSIs are raised, urban planners need to provide public open spaces and rights of ways for infrastructure.

Housing Problems Compounded by Rigid Land Regulations

Stringent land regulations—among their many effects—curtail the housing supply and make it less affordable and scarcer, though paucity of reliable and timely data makes it hard to calculate the shortages and the distribution across cities and income groups.

A range of estimates for housing shortages. Estimates for the country abound, ranging from 20 to 70 million units (Nenova 2010). A survey of slums carried out in the 65th round of the National Sample Survey (2008–09) points to 49,000 slums in India, 24 percent of them along *nallahs* (drains) and 12 percent adjacent to railway lines (National Sample Survey Office 2010).

To measure housing shortages, estimates of the population need to be switched to households (based on persons per household), and adjustments made to estimate the shortages due to overcrowding and poor housing conditions. In 2001, the census did this for all urban India. It estimated that the total number of urban households was 55.83 million, for an average urban household of 5.2 persons (288.4 million persons divided by 55.83 million households; figure 3.2). Yet it classified only 80 percent of the housing stock as acceptable, with the rest "*semi-pucca*" or "*katcha*"—housing in poor condition or built with semipermanent materials. The census also uncovered substantial overcrowding and building obsolescence. It calculated that 10.56 million more urban housing units were needed to relieve overcrowding, overcome obsolescence, and address poor housing conditions.

A few years later, a similar, partly retrospective examination suggested that housing shortages in urban India had shot up in 2001 from 3.0 million units in

Figure 3.2 Urban and Rural Population Trends in India, 1950–2050

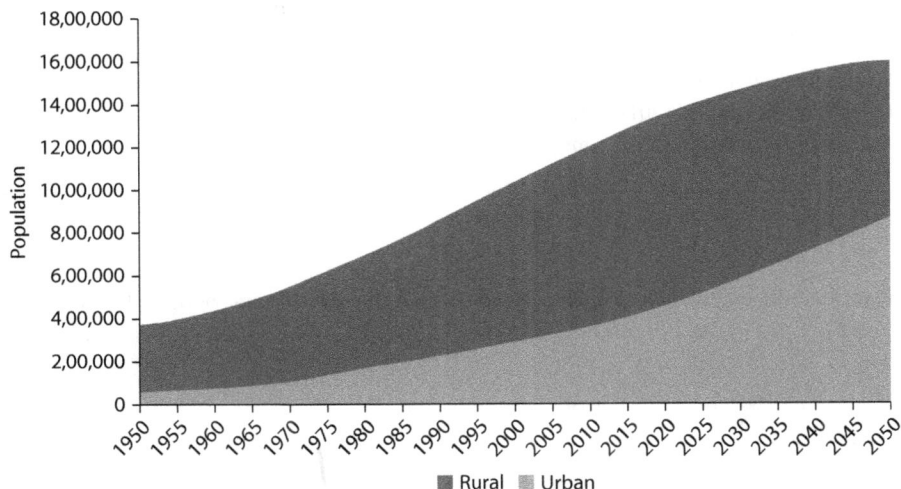

Source: Calculations based on United Nations data.

1971 to 7.0 million in 1981, 8.2 in 1991, and more than 24.7 million in 2007, and that urban areas needed to add 1.8 million units annually to accommodate new households. The Report of the Working Group for the 11th Five-Year Plan estimated that there were 66.30 million urban households and an urban housing stock of 58.83 million, giving a shortage of 7.47 million units. Of the total housing stock in 2007, "*pucca*" housing (units in good condition) came to 47.49 million units. The remaining stock was classified as *semi-pucca* (9.16 million) or *katcha* (2.18 million). The working group found that more than 19 percent of urban households lived in congested conditions (12.7 million), and estimated that 4.6 million units were either obsolescent or needed to be upgraded from *katcha* to *pucca*.

Even if one can quibble at the accuracy of these estimates, the housing market is just not maintaining its pace with household formation rates, keeping housing pricey and thus largely unaffordable to "economically weaker sections" and "low-income groups" of the population—around three-quarters of households in 2007 (table 3.2). Only a quarter are classified as middle- or high-income groups.

Across urban India, wealth—as measured by asset ownership—explains only 30 percent of the variation in housing quality. This is very low compared with Jakarta, for example, where wealth explains 62 percent of that variation. In Chennai, Mumbai, and Kolkata, wealth explains only 24, 22, and 19 percent of the variation in housing quality, respectively. And in Hyderabad, wealth explains barely 13 percent of the variation (figure 3.3).

Something is therefore disrupting the natural link between wealth and housing quality in Indian cities, most likely a combination of constraints on the supply of high-quality housing and of heavy congestion that leads households to sacrifice such housing to live closer to their jobs.

Table 3.2 Distribution of Households by Income Group, 2007

Income category	Estimated number of households (millions)	%
Economically weaker sections	21.81	32.9
Low-income groups (Rs. 3,301–7,300)	27.57	41.6
Middle- and high-income groups (more than Rs. 7,300)	16.92	25.5
Total	66.30	100.0

Source: Ministry of Housing and Urban Poverty Alleviation 2007.

Figure 3.3 Strength of Relationship between Household Assets and Housing Quality

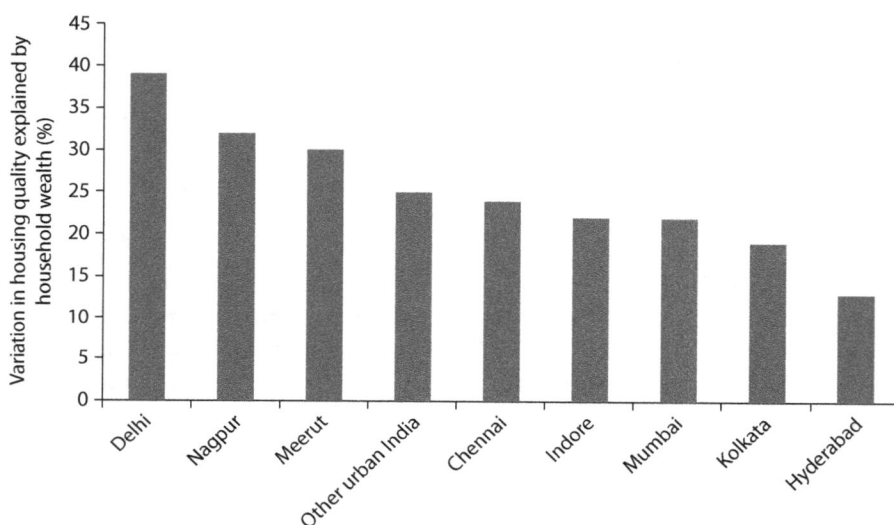

Source: Urbanization Review team calculations, based on data from a Measure DHS survey in 2005.
Note: This statistic was calculated using the following method. First, an index of housing quality was calculated, scored from 0 to 8 for each household, where 0 is the lowest quality housing, and 8 is the highest. Each household was scored—yes or no—on whether they had: electricity; water piped into their dwelling; a flush toilet either to the sewerage system or to a septic tank; permanent wall material; permanent floor material; permanent roof materials; three or fewer persons per sleeping room; and glass windows. Second, a wealth index was calculated, scored from 0 to 13 for each household, where 0 is the poorest and 13 is the wealthiest. It was calculated by scoring each household—yes or no—on whether they had: a radio; a television; a refrigerator; a bicycle; a motorbike; a car; a telephone; a mattress; a bed; a chair; a table; an electric fan; and a computer. Third, the housing quality index was regressed on the asset index for each of eight cities, plus a ninth regression for all other urban areas in the dataset, the Measure DHS survey, conducted in 2005. About 2,000 households were surveyed in each city, representative of slum and nonslum areas; 31,500 were surveyed in other urban areas in India.

Constraints to improving housing. India's urban housing market is impeded in myriad ways. The worst constraints include too little land for residential development, particularly for low- and middle-income groups; land use regulations that limit residential construction and redevelopment of older areas to higher density residential development; inadequate infrastructure to support residential development; high costs of construction materials; insufficient finance for construction; restricted mortgage finance; and rent control laws.

As scarcity of land, land use regulations, and infrastructure constraints have been discussed, we now look at some of the other factors.

Expensive building materials can result in expensive housing development. The National Buildings Organisation has pointed out the rising costs of construction materials—cement, rebar, roofing systems, and other building components. These costs have been rising worldwide,[9] and they are a critical determinant of housing costs (the other components are land, financing costs, and developer profits), directly affecting housing affordability, particularly for high-density housing. Developing new building materials and construction methods as well as better managing them can help hold prices down. Increased competition between residential real estate developers will also help to moderate housing prices.

Housing finance. Access to housing finance is very limited, and the lack of a well-developed system presents a particular barrier to low- and middle-income households entering formal land and real estate markets (figure 3.4). Indian buyers usually pay almost the entire price of the property before construction is completed (contrasting sharply with many other countries).

Rent control laws. Many cities enforce the post–World War II residential rent controls, keeping rents so low that landlords have abandoned their properties because the rental income does not cover routine maintenance. Mumbai, for example, has nearly 20,000 buildings that have been abandoned by their owners and taken over by the local government. Many of these buildings are so deteriorated that they pose safety risks to tenants. But more important, rent control laws have a chilling effect on the supply of new rental apartments. Developers rarely build rental units if there are rent controls because the controls make new construction unprofitable (Keating, Teitz, and Skaburskis 1998).

Figure 3.4 Weak Position of India's Housing Finance Market

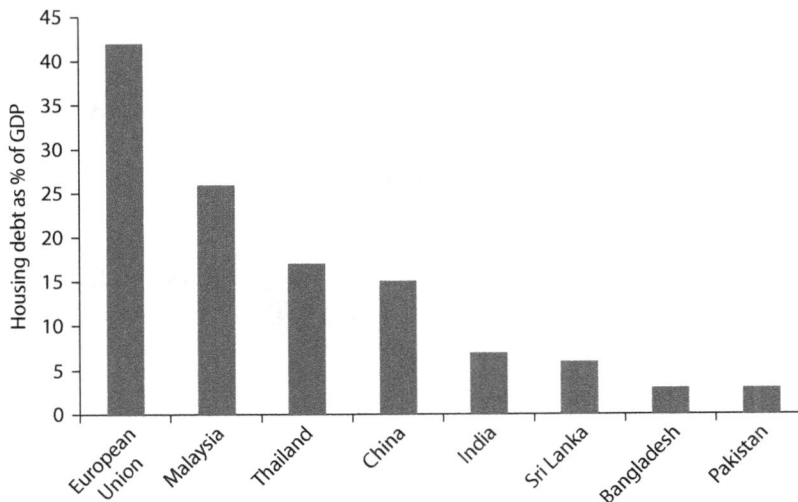

Source: Nenova 2010.

Box 3.4 Slums—A Rational Response from Individuals to a Lack of Affordable Housing

The development of informal settlements—or slums—has been the natural consequence of the constraints outlined above, and often represents an efficient response. The National Sample Survey Office's 2008–09 report on slums in 2010 provides a sobering picture of slum conditions across India and the costs required to upgrade these areas. Past approaches to slum improvement have been biased toward investment-intensive interventions, often demolishing settlements and resettling eligible households in subsidized new housing units.

The government's new program—the Rajiv Awas Yojana, launched in July 2011—brings a welcome focus to improving settlements where they are, and on tackling the root issues such as land market distortions rather than only treating their physical manifestation. New models of upgrading—how one integrates and involves stakeholders, how density is managed, how land rights are addressed, and how resettlement and compensation are managed—are key factors.

The Rajiv Awas Yojana also focuses on developing a rented social housing stock for new city entrants, an important step for many people to manage the move to an urban setting. The options include individual or shared rental units, as well as dormitories and night shelters for the homeless.

But upgrading alone will not solve slum problems. As long as housing and land markets are constrained, and housing prices outstrip affordability, slums will continue to grow across India. So slum policies need to reflect preventive and palliative dimensions. Upgrading with an expansive, responsive housing market would have the best chance of eliminating slums.

Source: National Sample Survey Office 2010.

Poor housing data at the national, state, and local levels. Finally, the timeliness, coverage, and accuracy of urban housing data are quite limited, making it very hard to frame effective policies and programs. The Reserve Bank of India has started developing a housing starts index from 2009. This is an excellent step in the right direction. Ideally, more statistical measures can be developed by the Ministry of Housing and Urban Poverty Alleviation and other central, state, and local agencies. With better information, policies can be more accurately tailored to real-world conditions and progress toward policy goals assessed.

One result of the above constraints is the proliferation of slums, which have heavy economic and social costs (box 3.4).

Challenges for Commuters and Freight

Urban land and building regulations are limiting densities in metropolitan cores and pushing people and firms to the outskirts of large metropolitan areas. As cities are forced to grow out instead of up, the urban transport network becomes increasingly important as the only way to connect people to jobs. A good transport system allows people to make efficient tradeoffs between the housing type and amenities they consume and the distance they travel to work. However, when the network is deficient, the problems stemming from stringent regulations in land markets are exacerbated. For example, people may be forced to live in slums if they cannot afford to move into formal housing nor access cheaper land on the outskirts of cities because of an inexistent or inefficient urban transport system. This section highlights the main challenges Indian cities face in urban transport.

Slow and Expensive Commuting

Slow commuting speeds and rapid growth of individual motorized transport. Congestion is a major challenge for Indian cities. Narrow roads and pervasive growth of private car ownership have slowed average journey speeds, so that motorized travel in all cities is barely faster than riding a bicycle (figure 3.5).[10] In addition, journey speeds in India's largest cities are typically more than 30 percent slower than in its smaller cities (figure 3.6).

Public transport has not been able to serve the expanding mass of urban commuters—ridership is relatively low—largely because of the lack of integration with feeder services and high costs. In principle, greater shares of public transport translate into greater sustainability of the transport system and lower use of scarce resources, such as land and fossil fuels.

Low ridership and often high costs of public transport. One metric of public transport ridership (across modes) credits Mumbai with a high share of about 45 percent, against Delhi's less than 20 percent—versus more than 60 percent in Moscow or 50 percent in Singapore (figure 3.7).[11]

Discussions between the Urbanization Review team and urban transport experts suggest that limited integration with other modes of transport, partly

Figure 3.5 Motorized Vehicle Growth Outstripping Population Growth in Cities

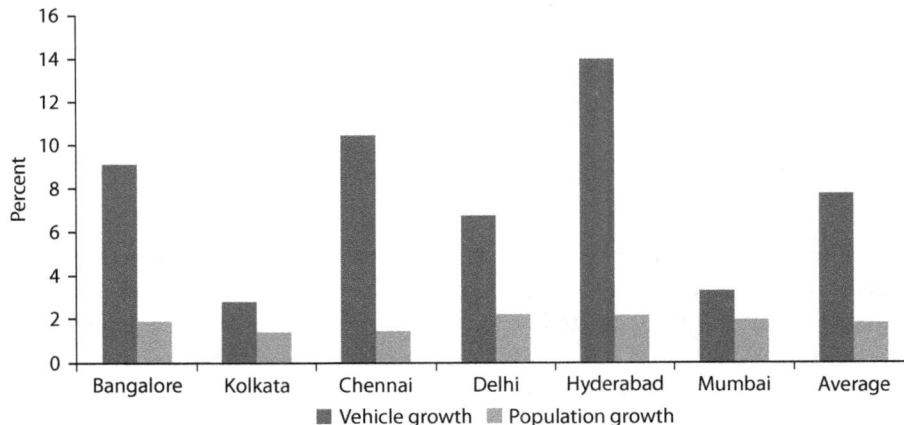

Sources: Ministry of Road Transport and Highways 2003; Ministry of Surface Transport 1999.

Figure 3.6 Average Journey Speeds during Peak Hours in Cities

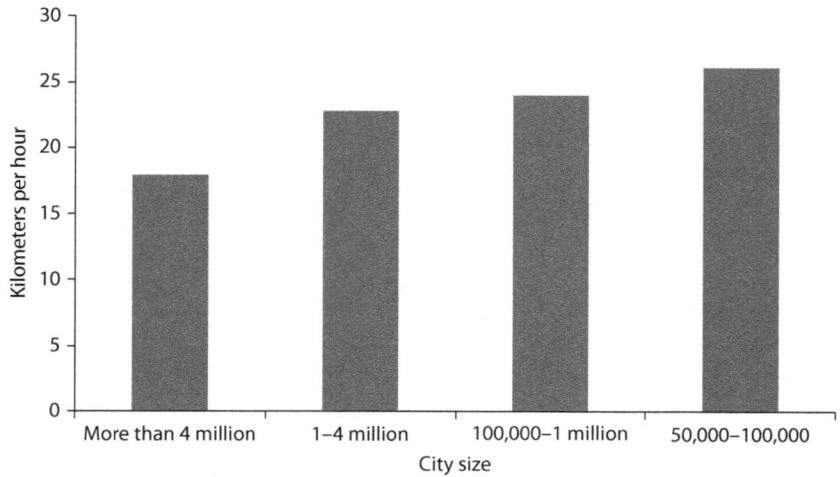

Source: Wilbur Smith Associates 2008.

Figure 3.7 Public Transport Ridership Ratios

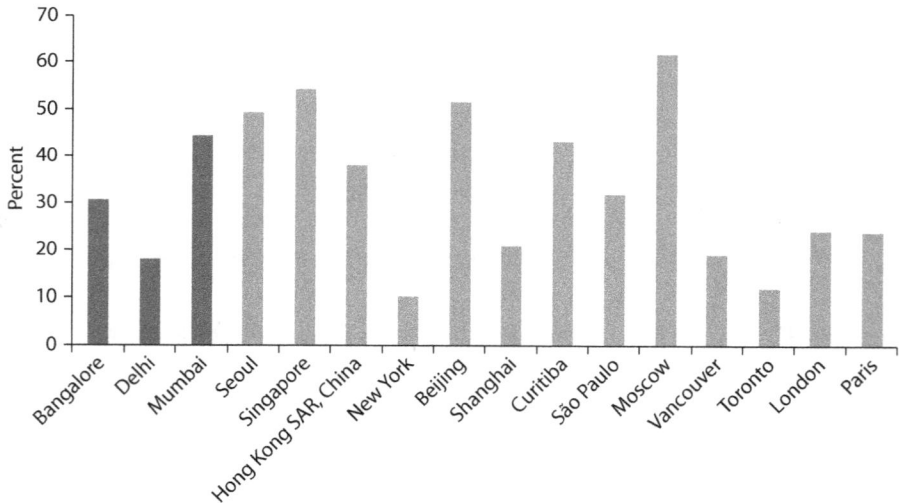

Source: Urbanization Review team calculations.

because of land use planning, is reducing the extent of public transport use.[12] The Delhi metro, for example—a global role model in construction and operations quality—is not well integrated with high-quality feeder services. Delhi metro carries only 6,520 riders per system km, much lower than Mexico City's 19,200, Moscow's 21,400, or São Paulo's 27,800.[13]

Low ridership can also be partly explained by the cost of public transport. Public transport in Indian cities is the least affordable among cities in a cross-country sample using a public transport affordability index, adjusted for per capita income (figure 3.8). Mumbai, for instance, is more than twice London and five times New York. Public transport in Hong Kong SAR, China, is the most affordable in the sample.

While affordability scores are largely driven by relative prices of public transport, public transport also tends to be less attractive and people tend to walk or ride a bicycle. But with small increases in income, people prefer to ride a motorcycle rather than ride a bus, as the marginal cost of using a motorcycle is much lower. In Delhi, petrol costs Rs. 50 per liter and, with mileage per liter on a typical motorcycle of 80 km, the marginal operating cost per km is Rs 0.60—against a cost per km of Rs. 1.50 for a bus and Rs. 1.80 on the metro. In addition, the convenience and social image of motorcycle ownership reduces the incentive to use public transport (despite the burden on congestion and pollution).

High Freight Costs

As urban transport is critical for connecting people with jobs in a city, an adequate logistics infrastructure is needed for city businesses to reach local, regional, and national markets. Market access provides the incentives for firms to increase production scale and specialize. India's infrastructure, inadequate to meet its burgeoning needs, constitutes a tight bottleneck to faster growth. Although India has recently embarked on a major program of modernizing its interstate infrastructure, it is uncertain whether the program is broad enough to address deficiencies in the rail system and to realize the potential of the country's waterways. Since the program is in its early stages, however, there is still time to extend it further and match supply with projected demand.

Figure 3.8 Public Transport Affordability Index

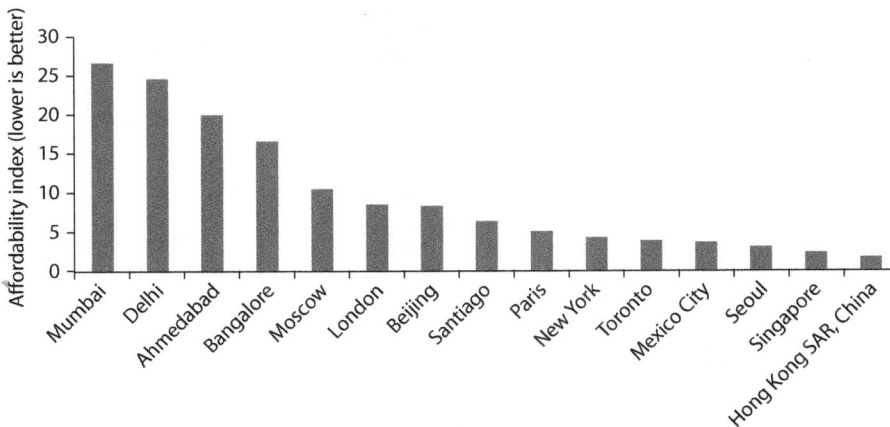

Source: Urbanization Review team calculations, based on purchasing power parity–adjusted data.
Note: The index reflects annual expenditures on public transport scaled by per capita incomes. Higher bars mean less affordable public transport.

Urbanization beyond Municipal Boundaries • http://dx.doi.org/10.1596/978-0-8213-9840-1

Indian industry spends 13 percent of GDP on logistics, whereas the figures for Germany and the United States are 8 and 9.5 percent, respectively (McKinsey Global Institute 2010). Much of this is attributed to excessive (57 percent) freight sent by road—especially relative to China—and too little by rail (36 percent) and water (6 percent), even though India is surrounded by ocean (figure 3.9). Even the United States—biased toward road haulage—has higher shares of rail and water. Because rail and water are potentially much less costly than roads and emit fewer greenhouse gas emissions, this wasteful pattern of freight transport is now analyzed more closely.

Around 65 percent of India's freight consists of bulk commodities and more than 75 percent is transported (in ton-km) over distances of more than 400 km. Bulk commodities can be transported over long distances much more cost-effectively by rail and waterways, while road is the least expensive for distances up to 400 km.

A special trucking survey, commissioned for this report, examined three route types (interstate movements between metropolitan cities, within-state intercity movements, and within-state rural–urban movements; see box 3.5). It finds that freight rates for short distances (less than 100 km) from large cities are on average Rs 5.2 per ton-km ($0.12; see table C.1). This is twice the national average of Rs 2.6 and more than five times that in the United States.[14] Self-reported total operating costs, combining fuel, salary, route allowances, and official and unofficial[15] overheads, were collected in the survey. They show a clear pattern: the operating cost profiles over different routes are proportional to the unit prices truckers charge, unsurprising given the very decentralized and competitive intercity freight transport market in India.

Figure 3.9 Freight Shares in India, China, and the United States, 2007

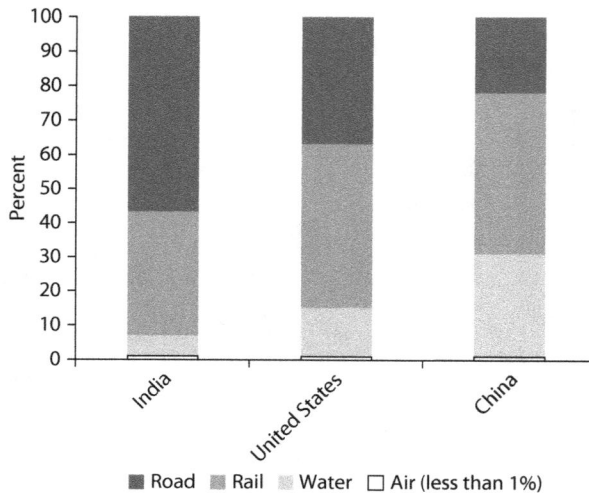

Legend: ■ Road ▨ Rail ▦ Water □ Air (less than 1%)

Source: McKinsey Global Institute 2010.

Box 3.5 Trucking Survey in India

India's intercity connectivity was assessed by a 45-route trucking survey commissioned by the World Bank (map B3.5.1; see table C.2).[a]

Map B3.5.1 Location of 45 Routes Surveyed in the Study

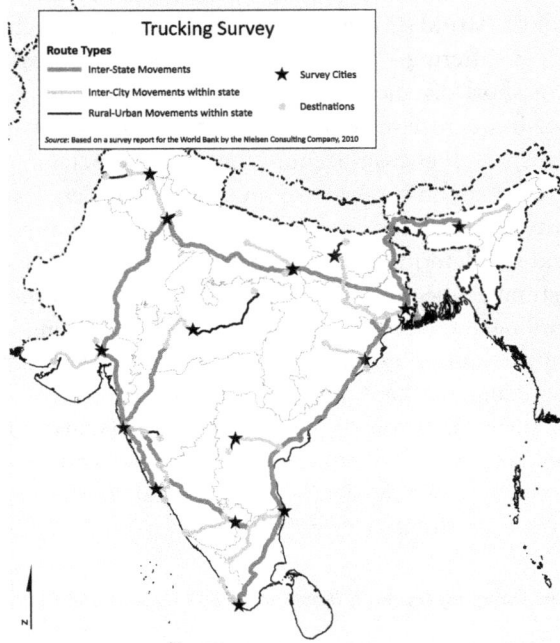

Source: Based on a survey report for the World Bank by the Nielsen Consulting Company in 2010.

India's intercity trucking industry consists of three components: transporters, truck operators (fleet owners), and brokers/agents. Transporters are trucking companies that offer front-line shipping services to shippers and customers. Truck operators, often called owner-operators, do most of the intercity freight transport activities. And brokers/agents liaise between transporters and truck operators and aim to ensure consistent, reliable services for transporters.

The larger and better organized trucking companies specialize in long-distance, interstate freight, and a plethora of small and uncoordinated operators serve shorter routes.

Source: Based on a survey report for the World Bank by the Nielsen Consulting Company in 2010.
a. The trucking survey was carried out by the Nielsen Consulting Company in 2010. The company interviewed 1,750 fleet owners and truck operators and collected route-specific freight transport information.

Much of the high, short-distance transport costs are due to use of smaller and older trucks on these routes as well as a higher share of empty backhauls as truckers often do not get a return load (see table C.3). In addition, trucks on short trucking routes run about 25,000 km a year, a quarter of what they need to do to be economically viable. The survey asked fleet owners what made trucks remain idle during a trip. Their replies represent the size of binding constraints for India's freight transport industry (figure 3.10). For all road segments and cities, lack of load or oversupply of vehicles is ranked the most critical constraint (41 percent nationally). Prices below breakeven point, another measure of market competition intensity, is second (32 percent). The results are consistent with findings of a World Bank report exploring transport issues (2005), which concludes that the pressure of a highly competitive market delivers to India's shippers some of the world's lowest freight costs, but that freight rates are so low that the industry is suffering a period of low profits or even losses (Bansal 2005).

The prices for short-distance freight movements are higher as truckers need to cover costs of frequent empty backhauls and large fixed costs. For interstate and intercity transport, fuel costs account for about 70 percent of total operating costs. For short distances on rural–urban routes, fuel costs are less than 60 percent of operating costs as wages and truck maintenance represent a larger share.

To understand the determinants of high transport prices for short distances, it is possible to estimate a regression using transport prices as the dependent variable and controlling for relevant variables. After controlling for trip distance, truck utilization (measured by yearly mileage) is the only statistically significant correlate for reducing the unit price of intra-urban freight transport. Other factors, such as the proportion of empty backhauls (which is correlated with truck utilization, size, age, and proportions of formal and informal facilitation payments), were tested, but no significant statistical association could be found for these variables with the determination of unit price.

Figure 3.10 Factors Delaying Trucking Movements by City Size and Route Type

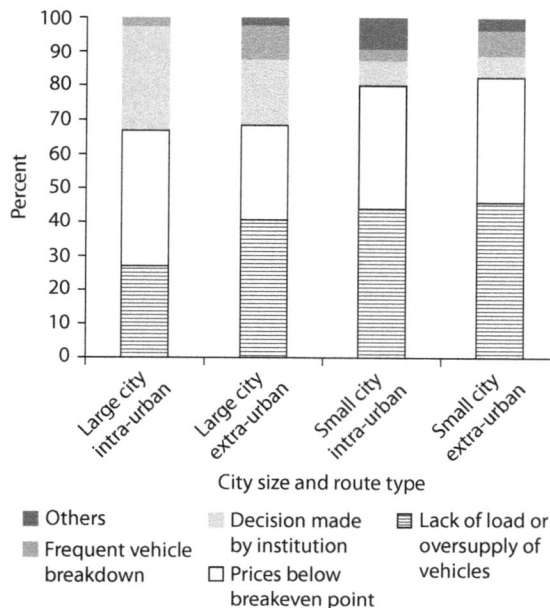

Source: Urbanization Review team calculations.

The Indian logistics system is also rife with inefficiencies deriving from poor infrastructure and equipment, high handling costs, theft, and damage. Hence, costs to users are much larger than in other countries at a similar stage of development. It has been estimated that India spends $45 billion more a year than required because of deficiencies in its logistics. Results from the transport survey suggest that improving the internal efficiency of truckers and trucking companies is likely to improve connectivity between cities and their suburbs. Adopting logistics management systems and creating trucking associations of truckers can help manage coordination failures and reduce the cost of metropolitan freight.

Spatial Disparities in Access to Basic Services

Just as affordable commuting and freight transport costs are central for integrating labor and product markets, good access and quality of basic services are important for the performance of firms and living standards of households. In this section, we focus on water and drainage, given their health externalities (though other services such as electricity are also key for city development).

Falling Coverage in Smaller Cities

India still has a long way to go in providing universal access to basic services and in equalizing access among different city sizes. The social landscape is highly uneven both nationally and within metropolitan areas. Disparities across the urban portfolio persisted at least until 2001, with cities above 1 million better off in all cases. The picture is even more discouraging in urban agglomerations, as the benefits of urbanization are not even reaching their outskirts.[16]

Access to basic services is best in the largest cities; it steadily worsens with declining city size, falling to the worst levels in rural areas (figure 3.11). Access to sewerage and drainage facilities worsens as city size decreases, with rural areas suffering from the lowest access levels. The gap in accessibility between rural and urban areas is large even for small cities. While urban areas have access of 50 percent or more, rural areas have 35 percent or less, depending on the measure used.

Access to drinking water is a bigger problem in smaller cities. For cities with more than 50,000 people, 60–70 percent of people have access to drinking water on the premises; for smaller cities, the share falls below 50 percent. Large cities have better water systems, with almost 60 percent of the population having access to piped water on the premises. Small and medium cities provide safe water at home to less than 50 percent of the population.

Service provision in large urban agglomerations also varies widely (figure 3.12). The seven cities with more than 4 million people are better off for access to services than smaller cities, but the disparity between the core of such agglomerations and surrounding towns is dramatic.

Figure 3.11 Access to Basic Services Worsens with Declining City Size

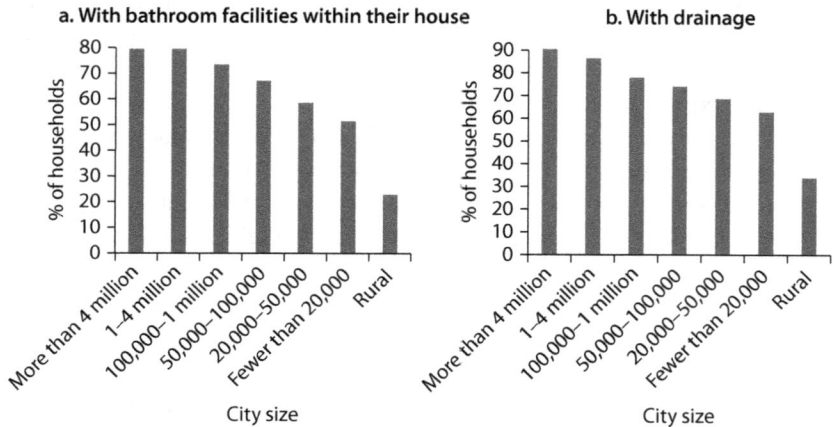

a. With bathroom facilities within their house

b. With drainage

Source: Ministry of Home Affairs 2001.

Figure 3.12 Share of Households with Access to Drainage

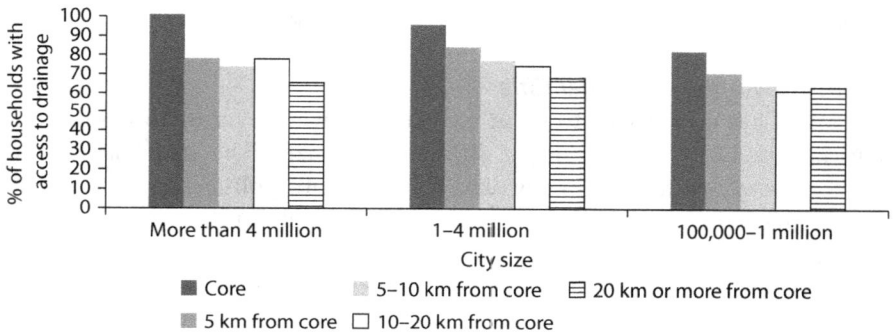

Source: Ministry of Home Affairs 2001.
Note: Benefits are confined to the core.

While 93 percent of households have access to drainage at the core, the dis-
advantaged fraction falls very rapidly with distance. Even for regions just 5 km
from the core, the share of households with drainage drops to about 70 percent.
Survey data from large cities such as Bangalore also show that access to network
services such as piped water is concentrated in the core, with access levels rapidly
dropping off toward the periphery. The disparities between core and periphery
are most acute for megacities. For cities between 100,000 and 1 million people,
even core access to services is limited, as about 25 percent of the population does
not have access to drainage (see figure 3.12). The benefits of urbanization are not
therefore spilling beyond the core.

Regional integration is crucial to achieving more evenly distributed and adequate quality-of-life standards, but to make the most of integration, normal
(market-driven) economic forces need to be identified and enabled. Equally,
spatial transformations must be promoted through planned development, and

the institutional and legal frameworks should be aligned to give the correct incentives for such transformations. The prosperity of cities must be extended to their neighbors. If suburban areas are integrated with the urban centers, the benefits from central cities will spill over boundaries, including access to social services.

Several factors drive the low access rates. First, lack of coordination between jurisdictions leads to fragmented provision of services that impedes economies of scale. Second, low tariffs do not allow for cost recovery and put strong financial constraints on utility companies, limiting their expansion capacity and hurting the quality of services. Third, low efficiency hits service capacity and unnecessarily increases costs of provision.

India's performance on water availability is disappointing compared with international standards (World Bank 2006). No major city in India provides more than a small percentage of its population, if any, with continuous water supplies. Yet in Jakarta access is 90 percent, in Manila 88 percent, and in Colombo 60 percent (World Bank 2006). In Delhi, 59 percent of industrial establishments experience low water pressure (World Bank 2007).

The larger point is that water supply is unreliable in cities, but the source of the problem lies in weak service delivery rather than insufficient availability, as seen by the fact that Coimbatore, Chandigarh, and Visakhaptnam register consumption of near 300 liters per capita a day.[17] This is slightly lower than in developed countries such as the United States where consumption is around 400 liters per capita a day (ADB 2007). That these cities have access to large quantities of water but cannot provide reliable service throughout the day points to serious policy and institutional distortions. The key issue is improving accountability to customers, increasing the autonomy of service providers, and providing incentives to deliver high-quality, sustainable services. This would require that policy makers take a fresh look at the governance arrangements and service provider models at the urban local body level and at the regulatory and oversight arrangements at the state level. As a first step, it is important to clearly delineate the role of various agents in infrastructure provision, maintenance, and service management. In most states, the roles of policy making, financing, and regulation overlap or are not properly defined.

Fragmented State-Central Government Institutional Responsibilities

Responsibilities are fragmented between central and state governments. The central government is responsible for regulating and developing interstate rivers and river basins (when such regulation is in the public interest). The Ministry of Urban Development is the principal agency of the central government that coordinates activities in urban water supply and sewerage; the Central Public Health and Environmental Engineering Organisation is its technical arm. The ministry receives assistance from the Ministry of Health and Family Welfare, the Ministry of Water Resources, the Ministry of Environment and Forests, and the Planning Commission. The Ministry of Water Resources has some responsibility for regulating groundwater, but no agency is the economic regulator for urban water supply and sewerage. The central government also sets the policy framework for managing water resources and provides funds for water supply and sewerage projects (World Bank 2006).

Apart from the above central functions, all urban water supply and sewerage matters are within the functions of state governments, which lay down policies for allocating water for different purposes and establish institutional systems for managing water. And such institutional arrangements vary from state to state. While responsibility for operation and maintenance (O&M) should theoretically be passed on to urban local bodies on completion of state-led infrastructure investments, lack of capacity and incentives among urban local bodies often leave state-level entities to carry out O&M functions (World Bank 2006).

Lack of coordination—among administrations and jurisdictions—increases inefficiencies. Coordination among various levels and functions of government is needed to unlock gains from urbanization. While public policies are often designed and (in theory) implemented within jurisdictional boundaries, the reality is that economic and social issues messily spill across administrative divisions. This often loses opportunities for getting higher returns from common institutions (such as harmonized environment and business regulations, arrangements for pooling natural endowments for common utility networks, and uniform tariff policies), connective infrastructure (transit systems to integrate labor markets), and targeted incentives (to reduce "beggar thy neighbor" competition). Coordination is especially important for services that cross regional boundaries such as water, sewage, transport, and land use planning. Effective systems of urban governance for metropolitan areas are also needed to ensure efficient service delivery (box 3.6).

Box 3.6 Coordinating Service Provision

Bangalore put through administrative reforms in 2007 to strengthen public service provision. With a relatively small peri-urban population, the metropolitan area seemed well placed to manage future growth sustainably. The idea was to improve service provision and management for a fast-expanding urban agglomeration, on the view that peri-urban jurisdictions were unlikely to provide services cost-effectively.

The Bangalore Municipal Corporation (BMP) was changed into the Greater Bangalore Municipal Corporation (Bruhat Bangalore Mahanagara Palike, or BBMP) that year, when it was merged with seven neighboring city municipal councils as well as 111 villages around Bangalore.

The BBMP is run by a city council, whose representatives are elected for five years from each of the 198 wards that make up the area. In addition to the BBMP, the Bangalore Metropolitan Regional Development Authority was formed as an autonomous body under the state government of Karnataka, to coordinate regional investment projects. In other areas, development authorities get involved in infrastructure investment, but in Bangalore, the Regional Development Authority focuses on planning, supervising, and coordinating the work of other

---

Box 3.6 Coordinating Service Provision *(continued)*

regional agencies: the BBMP, the Bangalore Development Authority, the Bangalore Water Supply and Sewerage Board, the Karnataka Slum Clearance Board, the Karnataka Power Transmission Corporation Ltd., the Karnataka Industrial Areas Development Board, and the Karnataka State Road Transportation Corporation.

Efforts are going in the right direction, but jurisdictions of several government authorities still overlap (table B3.6.1).

Table B3.6.1 Administrative Overlaps and Coordination in Service Provision in the Bangalore Metropolitan Area

Government body	Jurisdiction	Accountability	Tax collections	Water supply, sewage, irrigation, and drainage	Transport	Roads	Urban planning, development and control
Greater Bangalore Municipal Corporation	Bangalore Municipal Corporation and seven other municipal councils, as well as 111 surrounding villages	Citizens of corporations					
Bangalore Metropolitan Regional Development Authority	Metropolitan area	State government					
Bangalore Development Authority	Metropolitan area	State government					
Bangalore Water Supply and Sewerage Board	Metropolitan area	State government					
Karnataka State Transport Corporation	Metropolitan area	State government					
Private Buses and Paratransit Vehicles	Metropolitan area	Customers					
Infrastructure Development Department	Entire state	State government					
Indian Railways	Entire state	Central government					

Key agency in respective jurisdiction | Coordination | Overlap

Source: World Bank 2010.

Sustainability and Expansion of Services Undermined by Inefficiencies and Low Tariffs

User charges should in principle generate revenues that are at least enough to cover O&M costs and asset depreciation and to yield an adequate return on assets, and international good practice points to a minimum requirement to recover O&M costs from tariffs. Yet the operating ratios (O&M costs/revenue) for 20 Indian cities paint an alarming picture (figure 3.13).

Only a third of the water utilities cover their O&M costs. Among the rest, the worst performers are Indore, Kolkata, Mathura, and Bhopal, and for these cities, along with the other nine cities with operating ratios above 1, financial sustainability is a serious concern. (These 20 utilities may not, however, represent all urban local bodies.)

Beyond institutional improvements, utilities must enhance service continuity and introduce more metered connections. Only Nashik, Mumbai, Bangalore, and Coimbatore have at least 70 percent metered connections, Nagpur has 40 percent, and none of the others achieves even 10 percent.

Inefficiencies of water utilities in India are further confirmed by numbers of staff per 1,000 connections. International standards suggest that efficient numbers are around two staff members per 1,000 connections (McIntosh 2003). The average for the 20 cities is 7.4, far higher than globally efficient levels. This average also hides wide variations across cities: Ahmedabad, Rajkot, and Surat are near the global benchmark, but Kolkata and Mumbai have more than 17 per 1,000 connections.

Figure 3.13 Tariffs Fail to Cover O&M Costs of Water Utilities in Most Indian Cities, 2006–07

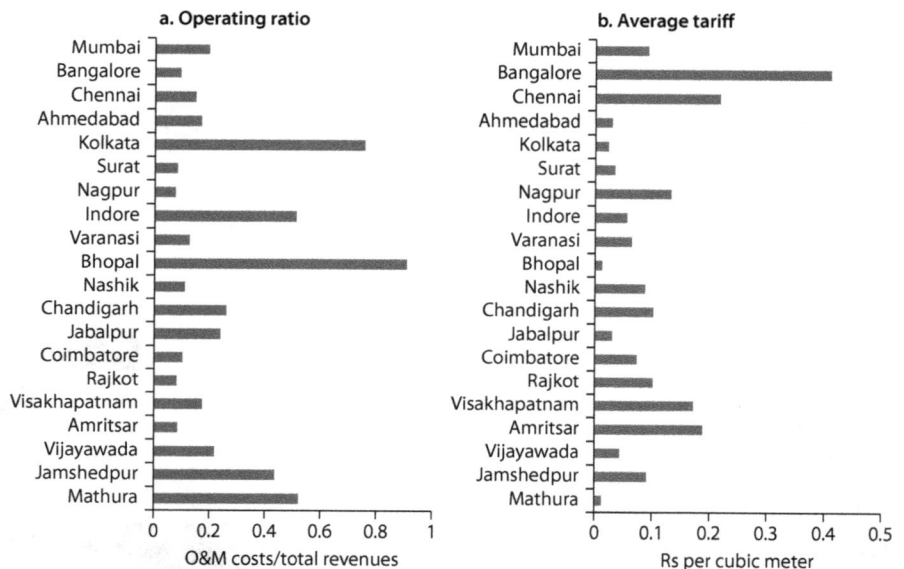

Source: Calculations based on World Bank's 2010 Survey for ULBs.
Note: An operating ratio less than 1 means that revenues from tariffs cover O&M costs; a ratio above 1 indicates that they do not.

If carried out well, 100 percent metering of water production and consumption, repairs of visible leaks, and reduction of illegal connections would vastly improve financial sustainability and lead to higher reliability and quality of services.

Average tariffs are also a good measure of the financial discipline of water utilities and their ability to recover operational costs from tariffs. Ten cities have average tariffs below the South Asian average ($0.09 per cubic meter), which in turn is lower than in other regions (Foster and Yepes 2006). Europe and Central Asia and East Asia and Pacific are the next highest, with average tariffs of $0.13 and $0.25 per cubic meter, then Latin America and the Caribbean at $0.41, almost 10 cents higher than the average for lower middle-income countries.

Despite relatively high tariffs, Amritsar and Chandigarh have very high operating ratios. These are probably explained by the very high rates of unaccounted-for water, of 57 and 39 percent, respectively, suggesting that efforts should be directed to this area.

Several studies in India show that households are willing to pay for improved access to water. A study on Bangalore looked at willingness to pay for additional days of water availability from direct connections, and estimated it, for an additional day a week of running water, at around Rs. 133 a month. Estimates from a contingent valuation survey confirmed these findings, suggesting a willingness to pay Rs. 134 for an additional day a week (Anselin and others 2010).

The major challenge is to increase access to reliable, sustainable, and affordable services. But the above analysis shows that the issue is not the willingness to pay or the affordability of services, but the efficiency and sustainability of services. Simply increasing access and creating infrastructure without addressing the management of the service may not lead to sustainable services. Investments in urban water and sanitation need to be accompanied by governance actions to enhance autonomy and accountability of service providers, improve incentives, and support professionalization. A recent World Bank report identifies the key elements of a statewide program for improving water and sanitation services and accountability, and financing mechanisms that can be linked to outputs or service improvements (or both) (World Bank 2012). For example, programs of the center, state, and urban local bodies can be linked to a mix of reform activities and delivery of service improvements (reduction of nonrevenue water, energy efficiency improvements, 24/7 water supply) rather than simply provide a source of finance to build assets.

Notes

1. Stamp duties are transaction taxes that are defined as a percentage of the property value. Stamp duties in India vary by state, running from 4.0 to 13.4 percent.

2. "Verordnung über Grundsätze für die Ermittlung der Verkehrswerte von Grundstücken," Werttax, www.werttax.de/downloads/wertv.pdf.

3. See chapter 4, the section "Institutional Foundations for Valuing Land."

4. Also known as the floor area ratio (FAR).

5. Findings from a model developed by Lin, Mai, and Wang (2004).

6. FSIs are only one instrument among a large set of planning tools, which include land readjustment, land assembly, development plans, infrastructure layout, zoning regulations, and height and bulk restrictions.

7. Commercial office districts typically have higher FSIs than residential districts.

8. With density bonuses, developers who want to put up an office building or hotel may be able to build a bigger and taller structure if they agree to provide affordable dwelling units in the building (referred to as inclusionary zoning in the United States), provide public art, or develop some of the lot area as a park.

9. There are signs that the rate is slowing.

10. Bicycles are typically ridden at speeds between 15 and 30 km per hour.

11. The formula is daily public ridership $\times$ 0.5/city population, measuring return trips.

12. Even though several initiatives are attempting to raise the supply of public transport.

13. Ridership data are from "City Pages," Metrobits, http://mic-ro.com/metro/selection.html, accessed, June 2011. All data are for 2010.

14. The national average obtained from the survey (Rs. 2.6 per ton-km) is consistent with Rs. 2.0 of the average financial operating cost of trucks (per ton-km) in Bansal (2005).

15. Informal payments.

16. Data for access to services come from the 2001 census. Census towns are grouped in six classes by population.

17. Chennai, Indore, and Rajkot are below the supply norms suggested by the Planning Commission of at least 150 liters per capita a day for cities with more than 1 million people.

References

ADB (Asian Development Bank). 2007. *Benchmarking and Data Book of Water Utilities in India*. Manila.

Anselin, Luc, Nancy Lozano-Gracia, Uwe Deichmann, and Somik Lall. 2010. "Valuing Access to Water—A Spatial Hedonic Approach, with an Application to Bangalore, India." *Spatial Economic Analysis* 5 (2): 161–79.

Bansal, Alok. 2005. *Issues in Freight Transport—India*. World Bank, Washington, DC.

BBC. 2011. "Panama's Towering Ambitions Strain Its Infrastructure." BBC News, July 18.

Bertaud, Alain. 2004. *Mumbai FSI/FAR Conundrum: The Perfect Storm—The Four Factors Restricting the Construction of New Floor Space in Mumbai*. http://alainbertaud.com.

———. 2008. "Options for New Alternatives for Development Control Regulation and Justification for Increasing FSI." Power Point Presentation, April, Mumbai.

Bertaud, Alain, and Jan K. Brueckner. 2004. "Analyzing Building-Height Restrictions: Predicted Impacts Welfare Costs, and a Case Study of Bangalore, India." Policy Research Working Paper 3290, World Bank, Washington, DC.

Cho, Man. 1992. "The Net Welfare Effect of Urban Spatial Growth Restrictions: A Closed City Model with Congestible Public Goods." Fannie Mae, Office of Housing Research Working Paper, Washington, DC.

Costonis, John J. 1974. *Space Adrift: Landmark Preservation and the Marketplace.* Champaign-Urbana, IL: University of Illinois Press.

Dowall, David E. 1992. "A Second Look at the Bangkok Land and Housing Market." *Urban Studies* 29 (February): 25–37.

———. 1998. "Making Urban Land Markets Work: Issues and Policy Options." Working Paper 702, University of California, Institute of Urban and Regional Development, Berkeley, CA.

Foster, Vivien, and Tito Yepes. 2006. "Is Cost Recovery a Feasible Objective for Water and Electricity? The Latin American Experience." Policy Research Working Paper 3943, World Bank, Washington, DC.

Fulton, William B., and Paul Shigley. 2005. *A Guide to California Planning.* 3rd ed. Point Arena, CA: Solano Press.

Ghatak, Maitreesh, and Parikshit Ghosh. 2011. "The Land Acquisition Bill: A Critique and a Proposal." *Economic & Political Weekly* 46 (41): 65–72.

Green, Richard, Stephen Malpezzi, and Kerry Vandell. 1994. "Urban Regulations and the Price of Land and Housing in Korea." *Journal of Housing Economics* 3 (4): 330–56.

Hannah, Lawrence, Kyung-Hwan Kim, and Edwin S. Mills. 1993. "Land Use Controls and Housing Prices in Korea." *Urban Studies* 30 (1): 147–56.

Keating, William D., Michael B. Teitz, and Andrejs Skaburskis. 1998. *Rent Control, Regulation and the Rental Housing Market.* New Brunswick, NJ: Center for Urban Policy Research.

Kertscher, Dieter. 2004. "Digital Purchase Price Collections—The German Way to Provide Transparency for the Real Estate Markets." Proceedings of the FIG Working Week, Athens, May 22–27.

Kim, Kyung-Hwan. 1987. "An Analysis of Inefficiency of an Urban Housing Market: The Case of Seoul." Doctoral Dissertation, Princeton University, Princeton, NJ.

Knapp, Gerrit J. 1985. "The Price Effects of Urban Growth Boundaries in Metropolitan Portland, Oregon." *Land Economics* 61 (1): 26–35.

Lafuente, Mariano. 2009. "Public Management Reforms and Property Tax Revenue Improvements: Lessons from Buenos Aires." Working Paper 0209, World Bank, Washington, DC.

Lainton, Andrew. 2011. "Decisions, Decisions, Decisions." http://andrewlainton.word press.com/author/andrewlainton.

Lee, Man-Hyung. 1999. "Green Belt Policy Change and Uninvited Aftereffect in Seoul." Chungbuk National University, the Republic of Korea.

Lin, Chu-Chia, Chao-Cheng Mai, and Ping Wang. 2004. "Urban Land Policy and Housing in an Endogenously Growing Monocentric City." *Regional Science and Urban Economics* 34 (3): 241–61.

McIntosh, Arthur C. 2003. *Asian Water Supplies: Reaching the Urban Poor.* London: Asian Development Bank.

McKinsey Global Institute. 2010. *India's Urban Awakening: Building Inclusive Cities, Sustaining Economic Growth* by Shirish Sankhe, Ireena Vittal, Richard Dobbs, Ajit Mohan, Ankur Gulati, Jonathan Ablett, Shishir Gupta, Alex Kim, Sudipto Paul, Aditya Sanghvi, and Gurpreet Sethy. New Delhi.

Ministry of Home Affairs. 2001. *Census of India: Census Data 2001.* Office of the Registrar General and Census Commissioner, New Delhi.

Ministry of Housing and Urban Poverty Alleviation. 2007. *Report of the Technical Group [11th Five Year Plan: 2007–12] on Estimation of Urban Housing Shortage.* New Delhi.

Ministry of Road Transport and Highways. 2003. *Motor Transport Statistics of India, 2001–02.* New Delhi: Census of India.

Ministry of Surface Transport. 1999. *Handbook of Transport Statistics.* New Delhi: Ministry of Surface Transport.

National Sample Survey Office. 2010. *Some Characteristics of Urban Slums, 2008–09.* Ministry of Statistics and Programme Implementation, New Delhi.

Nenova, Tatiana. 2010. *Expanding Housing Finance to the Underserved in South Asia. Market Review and Forward Agenda.* Washington, DC: World Bank.

New York City Planning Department. 2011. *Floor Area Ratio Variations across Manhattan.* New York.

Ohls, James C., Richard C. Weisberg, and Michelle J. White. 1974. "The Effect of Zoning on Land Value." *Journal of Urban Economics* 1 (4): 428–44.

Peterson, George E., and Olga Kaganova. 2010. "Integrating Land Financing into Subnational Fiscal Management." Policy Research Working Paper 5409, World Bank, Washington, DC.

Seidel, Carla. 2006. "Valuation of Real Estates in Germany. Methods, Transparency, Market Development and Current Aspects of Research." *Catastro* (Julio): 213–20.

United States Department of Labor. 2010. *Occupational Outlook Handbook, 2010–11.* Washington, DC: Bureau of Labor Statistics. www.bls.gov/oco/ocos300 .htm#oes_links.

Urban Redevelopment Authority. 2008. "Singapore Master Plan." www.ura.gov.sg/mp08/ map.jsf?goToRegion=SIN.

Wilbur Smith Associates. 2008. *Traffic & Transportation Policies and Strategies in Urban Areas in India.* New Delhi: Ministry of Urban Development.

World Bank. 2006. *Bridging the Gap between Infrastructure and Service. India Water Supply and Sanitation.* Washington, DC.

———. 2007. *Delhi Water Supply & Sewerage Services: Coping Costs, Willingness to Pay and Affordability. Bridging the Gap between Infrastructure and Service.* Washington, DC.

———. 2010. *Cross-Jurisdictional Service Provision in Indian Metropolitan Areas.* Washington, DC.

———. 2012. *India: Improving Urban Water Supply and Sanitation Service Provision— Lessons from Business Plans for Maharashtra, Rajasthan, Haryana, and International Good Practices.* Washington, DC.

CHAPTER 4

Priorities for Policy Reform

Introduction

Identifying options for accommodating urban expansion is gaining importance in India's policy discourse because 90 million people joined its urban ranks over 2001–11 and because existing cities are struggling to cope with infrastructure backlogs and regulations on development densities. Cities are projected to be home to another 250 million people by 2030. Given the structural changes in India's economy, cities will likely be increasingly important engines of economic growth—by 2030, they could account for 70 percent of GDP. Urban development is essential to enhance the efficiency of India's economy and to alleviate poverty. Investments and jobs created through urban development would in themselves be major elements of national economic growth and poverty alleviation.

Earlier chapters identified land policies and density management in cities, connectivity, and basic services as the key challenges that will uplift or undermine economic efficiency and spatial equity. Nurturing metropolitan economies can accelerate economic growth, and enabling other cities to flourish can improve spatial equity. Deregulating land markets and zoning practices, reducing the cost of freight transport, and extending access to such services as water and sanitation and improving their quality will be critical for progressing on both fronts. This section discusses how policy makers can think through their options.

Accommodating Urban Expansion through Land Policies

Institutional Foundations for Valuing Land

As India's policy makers work toward renewing existing cities and building new towns, they may want to acknowledge that land is a central issue that merits attention. Because economic transformation is changing land use demands, Indian cities will need to reorient their built environment. Getting urban planning right and setting the rules for land markets to be fluid is essential for economic prosperity. Today, land-market distortions in Indian cities hurt residents by lowering their standards of living while robbing firms of agglomeration effects that would lead to higher productivity. These losses, in turn, impede the urbanization process by making Indian cities look less attractive, and this slowdown further hinders advances in India's economy.

Strong institutions governing land use conversion, defining property rights, adjudicating disputes, and valuing land are necessary for land markets to function efficiently. Land valuation is in fact an integral part of land assembly for urban expansion as well as for local revenue generation because land values form the basis for property taxes, land sales, and leases. Developed countries have created systems to record and manage information on market transactions that serve as starting points in valuing land. However, these systems are often not available in developing countries, and transaction data are scarce or nonexistent.

A credible system that allows discovery and dissemination of land values is in place in countries where land valuation is successful. For this, three standardized techniques are used to enable appraisers to arrive at uniform, transparent, and independent valuations: the sales comparison, the cost approach, and the income approach.

The sales comparison approach relies on market data to analyze information on comparable properties. This approach is based on the assumption that consumers are willing to pay no more than they would for another property with similar characteristics (Gwartney n.d.). The reliability of the approach requires vast amounts of data, particularly transaction information on similar properties to that being assessed. This method is widely used where data in such volumes are available and are relatively straightforward to analyze, particularly with statistical software. It has two main weaknesses, however.

First, sales data may not accurately reflect transactions' market value, thus appraisers must understand the underlying factors of each comparable sale and adjust accordingly. Second, not all properties have enough market comparables (Gwartney n.d.). For example, in urban areas where undeveloped land is scarce, land sales are rare, resulting in few data on these transactions. While transaction data on built-up parcels may be available, decoupling land and built-up portions of a site is difficult. This form of analysis must often be paired with others to arrive at more accurate valuations. As with any land valuation method, this approach must be used with a clear understanding of the limitations of the underlying data.

The cost approach calculates land values by determining its residual cost once the land has been developed. The total development cost of the site is determined, including labor, construction materials, and infrastructure provision. These estimates also require understanding development restrictions based on area regulations as well as development potential given the market environment that affects the location and characteristics of the site. This method is complex because it develops values based on assumptions that require accurate knowledge of the following: land use restrictions; costs of inputs (labor, capital, and materials); fees and tax rates; sales price once developed; characteristics of the underlying land; and depreciation methodology.

Because this method is so speculative, it is often only paired with the sales comparison approach to justify that approach's valuation. Mixing approaches, in particular, allows for greater degrees of variation since they bring together several aspects of the market, many of which intersect. Additionally, the extent to which assessors analyze these markets may result in values that are difficult to determine objectively. In fact, these traditional methods of land valuation require extensive knowledge and data on real estate markets.

The income approach is applied to revenue-generating properties or lots of land, where income is divided by a market capitalization rate to arrive at a present value. This method is easily applied to rental property, where the net operating income is used to calculate annual income. The following is an example of how this is applied in practice. Assume that there is a piece of land generating $50,000 a year, and the determined market capitalization rate is 10 percent. The value of this piece of land is $50,000/0.1, or $500,000. While this approach seems extremely straightforward, it presents difficulties in arriving at a true valuation, including determining a reasonable capitalization rate or determining land rents in the absence of built-up property.

Getting around Institutional Weaknesses—Land Readjustment

While stronger institutions governing land use conversion and land valuation emerge and land markets mature over time, India's policy makers will need to act in the short to medium terms and may want to look at alternative options. Indian cities could thus explore expanding the use of land readjustment for land assembly and infrastructure development. Land readjustment is most commonly used to expand urban boundaries on the periphery of cities, but may also be used in urban areas for redevelopment (as in Mumbai's C-Ward).

Public acceptance of land readjustment. Land readjustment is gaining acceptance as an alternative to land acquisition as it has many advantages for land assembly. International practice is leaning away from land acquisition using eminent domain and toward land readjustment because it involves consultations with various stakeholders and because it does not require heavy upfront capital. In essence a participatory tool, land readjustment largely avoids the public discontent and protests that acquisition may generate. Land readjustment may thus be more politically feasible than acquisition in some situations—for example, when there is distrust among the parties involved. Because it is essentially a bottom-up approach it is also gradual, providing time to learn from the process itself. However, land readjustment involves efforts from public authorities, such as redrawing boundaries and adjusting property rights. Sometimes, land readjustment also requires local officials to initiate the project, as in Japan, and negotiate with affected landowners for a set of general agreements for the undertaking.

The premise of land readjustment is to provide public infrastructure at a shared cost to landowners and the municipality. This is achieved by assembling a readjustment area, providing infrastructure and basic services, and then reallocating land back to participating private landowners. The reallocation is based either on preadjustment land holdings or land values, but the land amount decreases on the assumption that the value of the land has increased through the provision of infrastructure. The land readjustment process allows land to be developed without the complex transactions characteristic of eminent domain. Rather than buying out all existing properties commercially or using eminent domain, the government agency can invite owners to participate in the project as capital investors. In return, owners are assured of receiving a property of at least equal value, near their original property, after the area has been developed. Landowners are more amenable to adjustment processes because they can stay where they are, preventing significant social and emotional ruptures that often accompany relocation. A potential issue is that land readjustment tends to ignore all those who derive their livelihood from the land but are not owners, such as tenants, squatters, or laborers.

Experience with land readjustment. While many countries practice land readjustment, its application is context specific. Before using it, countries must first assess whether they have the enabling institutions to facilitate their adoption of selected ideas from the approach. If the answer is no, a detailed plan to create such institutions is required. Countries must then ascertain what other institutions are required to operate a modified system that fits the specific context of the country. One of the most prominent international examples is Germany, perhaps the oldest model of land readjustment that has been replicated in many countries. Its success and acceptability are grounded in three main elements: well-defined property rights; streamlined, independent, and transparent evaluation processes; and a strong judicial system that addresses public concerns.

For its part, India has been experimenting with a variant of land readjustment exemplified in Gujarat's Town Planning Schemes. These borrow heavily from land readjustment in Germany and enable joint development between landowners and municipalities. Yet despite these programs' favorable reputation in India, they have not been used at scale outside Gujarat for a lack of enabling legislation.

Developing institutional foundations to support land markets is essential for the long term. Necessary institutions can be grouped in three types:

• Institutions that assign and protect property rights.
• Institutions that enable independent valuation and public dissemination of land values across uses.
• A strong legal framework supported by a healthy judicial system to handle disputes and oversee the process.

For land acquisition purposes, courts that provide guidance on the legal scope of eminent domain appear to be key institutions. Given that the definition of "public purpose" constantly evolves, having a rigid and exclusive list of the terms will pose stringent barriers to urban expansion. As an alternative, a flexible definition can be combined with a strong judicial system to guide and evaluate acquisition decisions case by case. But if a flexible definition is used, it becomes increasingly important to provide a clear definition of the process to adjudicate conflicts in cases where the public purpose of a particular acquisition is questioned, as well as to establish the institutions that guarantee that the affected parties can voice their concerns.

Strong institutions are required for land readjustment to succeed as a method of land assembly. If India's policy makers are to consider land readjustment methods for land assembly and as an initial instrument to defray the cost of infrastructure, they will first have to focus on evaluating whether institutions are ready to initiate the process, and then identify particularities of the local context that require changes to the international models of land readjustment.

Managing Urban Densities for Vertical Expansion

Just as assembling and valuing land are challenges for accommodating urban expansion, so are managing densities within cities and finding ways to finance urban expansion and city renewal. The debate on density regulation and floor space indexes (FSIs) should be placed in a broader urban planning framework that includes FSIs, zoning and use controls, height and bulk controls, and requirements for public space and rights of way.

The urban planning process is integrated in four domains (figure 4.1). It seeks to increase built-up space to accommodate people and businesses. Infrastructure is needed to support higher densities, but higher densities and greater infrastructure capacity increase land values, which can be tapped to generate revenues to pay for these investments—by levying property taxes and by using other land-value capture tools, such as developer charges or impact fees. If urban planning systems can link the four domains, they are well placed to promote economically vibrant and sustainable cities and metropolitan areas.

Figure 4.1 Urban Planning Cycle

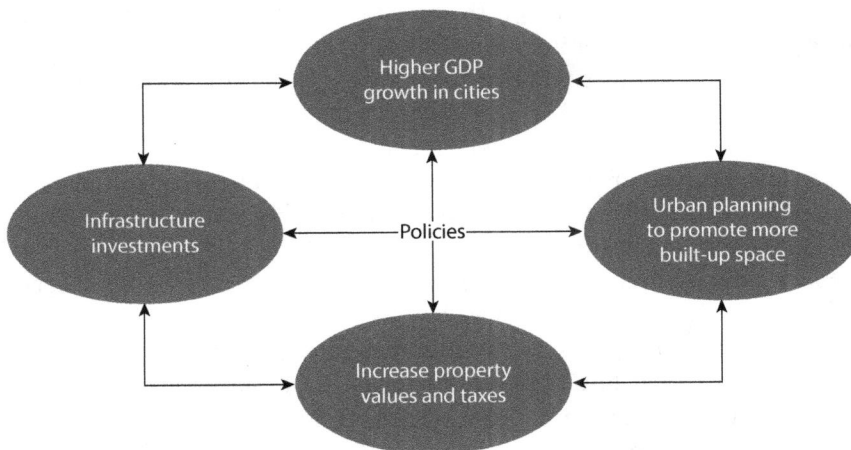

Source: Urbanization Review team.

International experience suggests that flexibility and granularity—or extremely local variations—are vital in land use regulations and density management policies. As in New York, FSIs vary by location as well as by land use. It also shows that FSI adjustments and infrastructure investments should go hand in hand. A good example is Singapore, where FSIs vary by location and type of use and by infrastructure availability: near metro stations, FSIs are typically higher because the transit system can accommodate the increased density and activity resulting from higher FSIs.

Improving housing conditions through land market reforms. Land regulations have implications for access to housing. Assuming an average household size of about five people, an extra 50 million new dwelling units will be required by 2030 (Ministry of Home Affairs 2001). This is in addition to the increases in the housing stock to address severe overcrowding and to replace dilapidated structures, estimated at 20–30 million units. So, India needs to construct 70–80 million units over 2000–30. This may take place through a combination of redeveloping existing residential areas to higher densities and developing new greenfield sites, the precise mix of which will be largely shaped by land use planning policies, regulations, and infrastructure availability. Higher density residential and commercial development will obviously foster more compact urban development, limiting urban sprawl and protecting arable rural land.

Increasing density and paying for infrastructure. São Paulo shows how a city can manage density while designing instruments to finance infrastructure. Before 1957, its urban legislation imposed constraints on the height of buildings, but these constraints were not enforced. Later on, in 1972, FSIs that varied by land use were introduced. And in 2000, a master plan changed the way of thinking: building rights became a government allocation. Today, this is a system of enhanced transferable development rights (TDRs), where low basic FSIs are combined with fees that allow building beyond the basic FSIs up to predetermined maximum FSIs.

India, too, has experimented with FSIs and TDRs to increase density along the Bus Rapid Transit corridor in Pimpri-Chinchwad. This is an example of how cities can increase densities while using land-based instruments to finance infrastructure improvements. The challenges include that development fees and TDRs are charged to developers, which may be seen as double taxation and may lead to lower development and high property prices and, perhaps, displace lower income households. Further, the use of TDRs is highly complex—increasing the need for supporting institutions.

Policy paths. As India embraces these challenges and prepares to change and update its institutions, policy makers can take one of two approaches—big bang or gradual. A big bang approach would implement drastic reforms, accelerating urban transformation, but it has high political, social, and technical risks. By covering the entire city at once, with zone-by-zone assessments and new regulations, the transformation could move rapidly once technical work is complete. But the process will generate much uncertainty and concern among stakeholders and planners. And because it is also a drastic and rapid reform, it implies lost opportunities from incremental learning.

A gradual approach may be easier to push through and lead to lower risks, and thus less political and social conflict. One way would be to start by selecting a couple of main streets and several areas around transit stations and developing higher density nodes in those areas, say, by increasing FSIs or selling TDRs (or both). India could experiment with different types and combinations of regulations and incentives and see how the market responds.

The gradual approach would also allow planners to experiment with various types of regulations and see how the market and the public respond. And it would also provide opportunities to develop social protection policies so that the poor are not hurt by the changes. During the gradual process, cities should curtail using TDRs and encourage real estate developers to focus on project areas—the selected main streets and areas around transit stations. If the gradual approach works, and stakeholders support it, the process could be accelerated gradually. A strong program of advocacy and awareness building for urban planners and policy makers to learn about new planning paradigms and to manage the higher densification can also help develop a cadre of skilled professions for this task.

Leveraging Accessible Locations with Coordinated Land and Infrastructure Improvements

Revive Existing Cities and Develop New Ones

India's urban evolution points toward increasing demand for the seven largest metropolitan areas and their suburbs. Other supporting evidence suggests that expanding information technology and related services will generate strong demand for office space in central business districts and new suburban centers, with the need to add nearly 15 million square meters of office space a year to keep pace with economic growth. Upgrading metropolitan cores and supporting suburban cities is likely to be economically efficient. However, it needs to be buttressed by institutional efforts that introduce flexibility in urban planning, land management, and land use regulations, as well as transparent land valuation and acquisition procedures that enable connective infrastructure improvements across the metropolitan area.

India's inclusive growth strategy may also call for setting up new cities to create jobs around smaller cities that have not yet been appreciated by investors. International experience highlights that new cities are likely to do well when near existing metropolitan areas, thus benefiting from economic and physical growth spillovers, as in the Shenzhen special economic zone of China (box 4.1) (World Bank 2008b).

But some countries have tried to create new cities without success, often because they failed to consider location, land policies, and connectivity. In the Arab Republic of Egypt, for example, the government developed 20 towns over 20 years to relieve the pressures of population growth in Cairo and the Nile valley (box 4.2).

Box 4.1 Success of the Shenzhen Special Economic Zone

The Shenzhen special economic zone was deliberately located just north of Hong Kong SAR, China. To enable land use transformation, the government acquired and assembled large lots of land for industry and housing, adjusting land prices to attract major industries while investing in the initial development of basic and connective infrastructure such as water and roads. Shenzhen was built on a greenfield site in a largely rural setting with only two urban settlements. The first was Luohu, the main customs checkpoint between the mainland and Hong Kong SAR, China, and a key gateway for people crossing the border by the Kowloon–Canton Railway. The other was Shenzhen Old Town, serving as a stopover for cross-border travelers.[a] Being a "city" planned from scratch, the government acquired and assembled large lots of land for industry and housing.

Land prices were adjusted to attract industries that the national government regarded as important for the country's economic growth. The introduction of a land market and the transfer of land use rights through auctions in 1987 led to a boom in property development and increased the extrabudgetary capital available to the local government to improve infrastructure and implement development plans. This helped the government develop basic and connective infrastructure.[b] As land markets were created and infrastructure provided, labor markets were also created, with Shenzhen being the first place in China to adopt wage reforms, including a minimum wage and a social insurance package. Companies in the special economic zone could write enforceable labor contracts with term limits.[c]

Shenzhen's proximity and links to Hong Kong SAR, China, enabled it to initially attract foreign investment in construction as well as labor-intensive activities outsourced from industries in Hong Kong SAR, China. Between 1980 and 1990, the central government invested only 1.4 percent of total physical development, and the local government 13.1 percent. Housing and infrastructure construction joint ventures with private developers (mainly from Hong Kong SAR, China) financed much of the physical infrastructure.[d] From 1980 to 2001, Shenzhen's population increased 14 times, fixed capital investment 488 times, GDP 724 times, gross output value of industry 3,014 times, and imports and exports 3,918 times.[e] Shenzhen is where the first foreign bank established a presence in modern China, in 1982; where the first post-1949 Chinese stock market was formed, in 1983; and where the first land auction took place, in 1987.[e]

a. Yeh 1985.
b. Zeng 2011.
c. Sklair 1991.
d. Yeung, Lee, and Kee 2009; Ng and Tang 2004.
e. Ng and Tang 2004.

Why the failure in Egypt? Distant location choices, overly rigid planning norms (escalating property prices and reducing the supply of affordable housing), and the lack of new connective infrastructure were crucial aspects. Critical too were plans to take development physically away from the largest metropolitan areas without enabling land and housing markets.

Box 4.2 Failure of the Arab Republic of Egypt's New Cities

Egypt's new cities were designed to attract industry and provide homes to people in pristine locations in the desert, away from the perceived dysfunction of Cairo. Starting in the 1970s, 20 towns were built and plans are being made for 45 more, making this the world's largest program for creating new cities. Industrial zones providing attractive tax incentives have also been created in these new cities.[a] Infrastructure financing for these cities accounted for 22 percent of the infrastructure investments of the Ministry of Housing, Utilities and Urban Development between 1997 and 2001.[a] Further, more than half the projects under the government's subsidized housing program have been directed to these new cities.

Yet infrastructure improvements to connect these new cities to existing metropolitan markets were scarce, providing disincentives for firms to relocate. Transport costs by road are $1.43 per vehicle-km in Egypt, well above the $1 per vehicle-km in, for example, Ghana, Lebanon, and South Africa.[b]

After more than 35 years of policies to support new cities planned for 5 million people, their population has barely hit 800,000. Nor have they deconcentrated the population from the Nile Valley and Delta, accounting for only 4.3 percent of national population growth in 1996–2006—an increase of just more than 1 million, dwarfed by an increase of almost 12 million in the Nile Valley and Delta.

The story is no different in the Greater Cairo Area. Eight new towns were created near Cairo but accounted for less than 14 percent of Greater Cairo's population increase in 1996–2006. Cairo's core agglomeration absorbed more than 50 percent of the total population increase in the area, and even peri-urban areas absorbed a larger proportion of the absolute increase (about 36 percent) than the new towns.

a. World Bank 2008a.
b. Nathan Associates 1999.

New Cities Are Not an Escape from Metropolitan Challenges

International experience suggests that developing cities is more risky when they are distant from major metropolitan areas (as in Egypt). So, before planning new towns around distant places, India's government should assess why these other places have not taken off. Is it because of regulatory constraints, high transport costs, or low market accessibility that reduces the private returns to investment? If public investments are made to offset some of these costs, will they be successful in countering the tendency of firms to cluster in sectors that value agglomeration economies? And, since agglomeration economics imply that some metropolitan concentration of economic activity is optimal for productivity, the tradeoff between national efficiency in industrial location and spatial equity needs to be considered.

The policy challenge is not one of creating new cities at the expense of existing metropolitan areas. In any case, people and jobs are flowing from metropolitan cores to nearby settlements, regardless of whether the settlements are classified as urban or rural. The challenge is to ensure that new cities and existing metropolises are connected and land use change is coordinated with infrastructure development to accommodate urban redevelopment and urban spatial expansion.

While the seven largest cities in the country have the highest concentration of economic activities that benefit from agglomeration economies—such as information and communication technology services and high-tech manufacturing—they have stagnated in recent years. Between 1993 and 2006, they failed to increase their overall shares in national employment, or even in employment in the above economic activities. International experience—that metropolitan concentration increases until per capita income reaches $7,000–10,000—suggests that the liberalization of industrial investment decisions in the 1990s should have led to greater economic concentration in India's metropolitan areas.

The suburbs of large metropolitan areas in India are well suited for a first round of *new city* efforts. However, India's largest cities today lack the infrastructure needed to make cities more efficient, and efforts to renew existing cities are required to support growth. Upgrading existing cities is thus important even when new cities are being built.

Efforts to manage urban expansion will be dampened unless underlying land market distortions are corrected, investments are made to set aside rights of way for infrastructure, and infrastructure is developed in areas already showing economic promise. Irrespective of whether urban regeneration or new city development is pursued, the underlying preconditions of fluid land markets and connective infrastructure remain important.

Enhancing Connectivity and Service Delivery—Establishing the Rules of the Game

Addressing the challenges India faces in developing urban areas and providing infrastructure requires efforts on numerous fronts. Because economic transformation is changing land use demands, Indian cities need to reorient their built environment. To accommodate urban expansion, India needs to make changes to its urban planning license raj. Getting urban planning right is essential for economic prosperity. But Indian cities also lack adequate infrastructure, and new infrastructure is needed to make them more efficient. Recent studies by HPEC (2011) and McKinsey Global Institute (2010) estimate that $0.9–2.2 trillion is needed to improve infrastructure in existing towns. Public investment to improve urban infrastructure can best attract and sustain firms and households when it is consistent with the economic potential of places.

Coordinating land use transformation with infrastructure improvement is one of the key challenges for Indian cities. Redeveloping existing cities and accommodating demand for urban expansion is equally important. The challenge—and potential opportunity—is that population densities in and around the largest metropolitan areas are extremely high, averaging 2,450 persons per square kilometer in the 50 km vicinity of the largest metropolises, while a third of India's new towns were born in a 50 km neighborhood of existing cities with more than 1 million people. If these trends are any indication of how the future will unfold, much of India's urbanization challenge will be to transform land use and expand infrastructure in its largest cities and neighboring suburbs—places that are not pristine or greenfield but that already support 9 percent of the country's population and provide 18 percent of employment on 1 percent of the country's land area. The problem so far has been that high population densities have not been accompanied by commensurate substitution between scarce land and durable capital or built-up area.

For housing, cities and metropolitan areas should consider a comprehensive reform of land use regulations to bring flexibility to their urban structure plans. They should also ensure that the reformed regulations are aligned with forecast economic and demographic growth, keeping close attention on supporting both outward expansion and increased density in urbanized areas. Further, coordinating land use planning with infrastructure provision is essential. States and cities should develop sustainable models for financing infrastructure and public service requirements to support higher densities, using such tools as property taxation, development impact fees and charges, and land value capture.

Enhancing connectivity between and within cities will be key for economic growth. Reductions in transport costs are likely to increase the interaction between cities and facilitate spatial transformations. In particular, reductions in the costs of moving goods for short trips around large metropolitan areas are likely to have the largest impact because they will improve connectivity between places with high population growth and increasing economic activity. Within-city connectivity is also important to shorten the distance between people and jobs.

With basic services, connection levels vary by city size—higher in larger cities—but even here reliability is extremely low. Solving issues of overlapping functions at different levels of government, improving coordination of government levels and providers, plugging water leakages, and increasing water metering are ways to move toward universal and reliable access. Yet even within large cities and neighboring areas, access to basic services declines rapidly with distance from the center, locking in the benefits of urbanization in the core. Understanding the main issues that lead to this progressive spatial deterioration is important so that effective solutions can be provided. Recent analysis shows the need for autonomous, accountable, and professional service providers, along with appropriate incentives and capacity-building programs, to address the inefficiencies in the urban water and sanitation sector.

Policy makers should also consider other issues. First, they should think about laying the foundations for competition and cost recovery. As valuation is important for land acquisition, this report has stressed the importance of pricing for basic services, transport, and other infrastructure. Cost-covering prices are essential to improve the sustainability of services. In some cases, subsidies could be considered to enhance access for specific groups of the population for which equity is a concern, though they should be transparent, targeted, linked to performance, and time-limited. Output-based aid may be an alternative (box 4.3). But overall, average tariffs should cover all costs, including capital and expansion costs.

Box 4.3 Cambodian Water Subsidies

A subsidy designed to increase the connectivity to piped water can be tied to the number of new connections. In Cambodia, affordability concerns led to the use of a subsidy for water connections targeting low-income households.

The price offered per connection was about 25 percent below the original price. And the operator receives a payment based on the actual delivery of the new connection. Each new connection is inspected by an independent engineer before payment to the operator is made. The output-based aid is funded through a credit from the International Development Association.

Sources: Mumssen 2004; World Bank 2006.

When tariffs cover these costs, the right incentives for providers (private or public) to deliver and expand infrastructure services are in place.

Second, policy makers should provide the incentives for coordination across jurisdictional boundaries and administrative units. Interjurisdictional coordination allows economies of scale to be exploited in service provision. International experience suggests that flexible rules allow cities to respond to changing conditions by reforming interjurisdictional arrangements. Cities like Toronto with clear but flexible rules have responded to changing pressures of urbanization by adapting the interjurisdictional arrangements for service provision. In particular, it moved from a one- to two-tiered government in the 1950s, created a metropolitanwide coordination office in the 1970s, and finally amalgamated municipal arrangements under one City of Toronto in the 1980s. Provincewide and sector-specific entities such as the Greater Toronto Transportation Authority have been introduced and reformed over time. Incentives for cooperation through established and recognized authorities are key for efficiently providing basic services (World Bank 2011).

Managing India's spatial transformation will have a considerable bearing on economic efficiency and social equity. This report provides diagnostics on the pace and form of spatial transformation, documents key policy distortions in land, housing, and infrastructure that curtail the benefits and pace of transformation, and identifies options for policy, drawing on international experience.

References

Gwartney, Ted. n.d. "Estimating Land Values." www.henrygeorge.org/ted.htm.

HPEC (High Powered Expert Committee). 2011. *Report on Indian Urban Infrastructure and Services.* Government of India, New Delhi.

McKinsey Global Institute. 2010. *India's Urban Awakening: Building Inclusive Cities, Sustaining Economic Growth,* by Shirish Sankhe, Ireena Vittal, Richard Dobbs, Ajit Mohan, Ankur Gulati, Jonathan Ablett, Shishir Gupta, Alex Kim, Sudipto Paul, Aditya Sanghvi, and Gurpreet Sethy. New Delhi.

Ministry of Home Affairs. 2001. "Census of India: Census Data 2001." Office of the Registrar General and Census Commissioner, New Delhi.

Mumssen, Yogita. 2004. "Output-based Aid in Cambodia: Private Operators and Local Communities Help Deliver Water to the Poor." Note 1, The Global Partnership on Output-Based Aid, Washington, DC.

Nathan Associates. 1999. *Reducing Transport Costs of Egypt's Exports.* U.S. Agency for International Development, Cairo.

Ng, Mee Kam, and Wing-Shing Tang. 2004. "The Role of Planning in the Development of Shenzhen, China: Rhetoric and Realities." *Eurasian Geography and Economics* 45 (3): 190–211.

Sklair, Leslie. 1991. "Problems of Socialist Development—the Significance of Shenzhen Special Economic Zone for China Open-Door Development Strategy." *International Journal of Urban and Regional Research* 15 (2): 197–215.

World Bank. 2006. *Bridging the Gap between Infrastructure and Service. India Water Supply and Sanitation.* Washington, DC.

———. 2008a. *Arab Republic of Egypt, Urban Sector Update* (Vols I and II). Sustainable Development Department, Middle East & North Africa Region, Cairo.

———. 2008b. *World Development Report 2009: Reshaping Economic Geography.* Washington, DC.

———. 2011. *Urbanization Review—Colombia.* Washington, DC: Finance, Economics, and Urban Department, Urban and Local Governments Unit.

Yeh, Anthony Gar On. 1985. "Development of the Special Economic Zone in Shenzhen, The People's Republic of China." *Ekistics* (March/April): 154–61.

Yeung, Yue-man, Joanna Lee, and Gordon Kee. 2009. "China's Special Economic Zones at 30." *Eurasian Geography and Economics* 50 (2): 222–40.

Zeng, Douglas Zhihua. 2011. "How Do Special Economic Zones and Industrial Clusters Drive China's Rapid Development?" Policy Research Working Paper 5583, World Bank, Washington, DC.

APPENDIX A

India's Urbanization Trends

Table A.1 Urban Population Distribution: Historical Overview

	City size						
	More than 4 million	1–4 million	100,000–1 million	50,000–100,000	20,000–50,000	Fewer than 20,000	Total
Total urban population, 2001 (millions)	65.1	42.2	89.1	27.8	35.2	26.8	286.1
Share (%)	22.7	14.8	31.1	9.7	12.3	9.4	100.0
Share change, 1901–2001, (percentage points)	8.6	2.2	–3.0	–5.2	–5.0	2.4	0.0
Total urban population, 1951 (millions)	11.2	7.5	18.1	7.1	7.7	3.1	54.7
Share (%)	20.4	13.7	33.2	12.9	14.1	5.6	100.0
Total urban population, 1901 (millions)	3.3	2.9	7.9	3.5	4.0	1.6	23.2
Share (%)	14.2	12.6	34.1	14.9	17.3	6.9	100.0

Source: Population censuses.

Table A.2 Urban Population Growth across City Sizes
%, unless otherwise indicated

	City size						
Annual city population growth	More than 4 million	1–4 million	100,000–1 million	50,000–100,000	20,000–50,000	Fewer than 20,000	Total
1981–91	3.14	3.70	3.31	2.58	2.71	2.35	3.14
1991–2001	3.09	3.38	2.93	2.40	2.28	1.88	2.84
Share change, from 1981–91 to 1991–2001 (percentage points)	–0.05	–0.32	–0.38	–0.19	–0.43	–0.47	–0.30
1971–81	3.40	4.11	3.86	3.43	3.18	2.55	3.62
1901–71	2.70	2.38	2.18	1.56	1.13	0.73	2.18

Source: Population censuses.

Table A.3 The Share of Urban Population in Multiple Ring Buffers from the National Railway System, 1901–2001

percent

	Distance from railway						
	Fewer than 10 km	*10–20 km*	*20–30 km*	*30–40 km*	*40–50 km*	*More than 50 km*	*Total*
1901	81.8	11.2	2.9	1.2	0.8	2.1	100.0
1911	82.5	10.2	2.8	1.2	0.8	2.5	100.0
1921	83.2	9.8	2.9	1.1	0.8	2.3	100.0
1931	83.5	9.4	2.9	1.1	0.8	2.3	100.0
1941	84.7	8.7	2.8	0.9	0.7	2.1	100.0
1951	86.2	7.9	2.6	0.9	0.7	1.8	100.0
1961	87.3	7.0	2.6	0.8	0.6	1.8	100.0
1971	87.3	6.9	2.5	0.8	0.6	1.8	100.0
1981	86.0	7.8	2.6	0.8	0.7	2.1	100.0
1991	86.0	8.1	2.6	0.9	0.7	1.7	100.0
2001	84.6	8.9	2.6	0.9	0.7	2.2	100.0
Share change, 1901–2001 (percentage points)	2.8	−2.3	−0.4	−0.2	−0.1	0.1	0.0

Source: Population censuses.
Note: The share of land area within 10 km from railways is 30.4 percent.

Table A.4 The Share of Urban Population in Multiple Ring Buffers from the National Highway System, 1901–2001

percent

	Distance from national highway						
	Fewer than 10 km	*10–20 km*	*20–30 km*	*30–40 km*	*40–50 km*	*More than 50 km*	*Total*
1901	55.1	11.8	7.7	5.5	4.7	15.1	100.0
1911	56.3	11.7	7.5	5.1	4.6	14.9	100.0
1921	56.9	11.7	7.7	4.8	4.5	14.3	100.0
1931	57.2	11.5	7.5	4.8	4.5	14.5	100.0
1941	59.3	11.1	7.3	4.4	4.1	13.8	100.0
1951	60.9	11.0	6.7	4.1	3.9	13.3	100.0
1961	64.1	10.1	6.3	3.7	3.5	12.2	100.0
1971	64.6	10.3	6.1	3.6	3.3	12.1	100.0
1981	62.8	11.0	6.7	3.7	3.3	12.5	100.0
1991	62.9	11.5	6.1	3.6	3.1	12.8	100.0
2001	63.0	12.1	5.9	3.5	3.0	12.4	100.0
Share change, 1901–2001 (percentage points)	7.9	0.3	−1.8	−2.0	−1.7	−2.7	0.0

Source: Population censuses.

Table A.5 Changing Urban Systems toward Broadly Defined Urban Sprawl

	2001	2011	Growth, 2001–11 (%)
Number of administrative units			
Towns	5,161	7,935	53.7
Statutory towns	3,799	4,041	6.4
Census towns	1,362	3,894	185.9
Villages	638,588	640,867	0.4
Population (millions)			
Urban	286.1	377.1	31.8
Rural	742.6	833.1	12.2
Average settlement size			
Urban (population per town)	55,439	47,524	−14.3
Rural (population per village)	1,163	1,300	11.8

Sources: Ministry of Home Affairs 2001 and 2011.

Table A.6 New Town Birth, 1991–2001

	Distance from the nearest city of more than 1 million people						
	Fewer than 50 km	50–100 km	100–200 km	200–300 km	300–450 km	More than 450 km	Total
New towns, 1991–2001	269	203	384	140	72	40	1,108
Towns in 1991	780	752	1,401	641	269	210	4,053
New town birth rate (%)	34.5	27.0	27.4	21.8	26.8	19.0	27.3

Sources: Ministry of Home Affairs 1991 and 2001.

Table A.7 Urban Amenities across City Sizes

	City size						
	More than 4 million	1–4 million	100,000–1 million	50,000–100,000	20,000–50,000	Fewer than 20,000	Total
Natural geography							
Average rainfall (mm)	1,349	923	1,114	1,036	1,072	1,141	1,129
Temperature, maximum (Celsius)	35.2	37.1	37.7	37.6	37.2	36.5	36.9
Temperature, minimum (Celsius)	17.0	14.1	14.4	14.6	14.3	14.9	15.0
Business amenities							
Distance to railway station (km)	1.8	1.1	6.7	16.3	19.4	27.6	9.1
Population density (per sq. km)	17,460	7,944	7,342	5,925	4,486	3,434	8,884
Illiteracy rate (%)	26.0	29.1	29.9	33.3	35.7	36.1	30.5
Local roads (km per 100,000 people)	62.7	104.9	111.3	107.6	173.0	173.9	112.4
Local roads (km per sq. km area)	9.0	7.1	7.7	5.6	5.8	4.7	7.2
Power connection (per 10 people)	1.8	3.5	1.8	1.8	1.7	1.8	2.1
Banks and credit societies (per 100,000 people)	27.7	33.3	35.1	33.2	40.3	44.8	34.5

table continues next page

Table A.7 Urban Amenities across City Sizes *(continued)*

	City size						
	More than 4 million	1–4 million	100,000–1 million	50,000–100,000	20,000–50,000	Fewer than 20,000	Total
Consumer amenities							
Health clinic beds (per 100,000 people)	250.0	267.8	328.2	286.3	323.6	296.4	293.6
Schools (per 100,000 people)	55.7	60.8	70.4	79.7	90.0	112.3	72.9
Cultural facilities (per 100,000 people)	6.5	11.8	16.0	19.5	24.5	33.4	15.9

Source: Population censuses.

Table A.8 Business Services and ICT Concentrate in the Largest Cities, Low-End Manufacturing and Personal Services Are Dispersed

location quotient

	City size					
	More than 4 million	1–4 million	100,000–1 million	50,000–100,000	20,000–50,000	Fewer than 20,000
ICT services	2.09	1.00	0.71	0.27	0.27	0.19
Financial services	1.16	1.02	1.02	0.88	0.82	0.73
Real estate	1.65	0.97	0.79	0.67	0.60	0.54
Manufacturing						
High tech	1.39	1.41	0.69	0.62	1.00	0.48
Fast-growing export	1.33	1.17	0.81	0.88	0.75	0.77
Medium high tech	1.13	1.60	0.77	0.94	0.77	0.70
Medium low tech	1.18	1.30	0.89	0.77	0.79	0.79
Low tech	1.01	1.06	0.97	1.04	0.99	0.94
Utilities (electricity, gas, and water)	0.90	0.84	0.95	1.04	1.17	1.61
Construction	0.99	1.04	1.10	0.93	0.84	0.89
Transport, telecom	1.23	0.94	0.98	0.87	0.83	0.75
Public administration	0.64	0.93	1.21	1.21	1.17	1.10
Education	0.85	0.97	1.06	1.01	1.08	1.25

Source: Calculations based on Ministry of Statistics and Programme Implementation 2005.

Table A.9 Location of Employment in Multiple Ring Buffers from the Big Seven Cities

	Distance from the center						
	Fewer than 50 km	50–100 km	100–200 km	200–300 km	300–450 km	More than 450 km	Total
Total workers							
National share (%)	17.5	5.2	15.5	18.3	19.7	23.8	100.0
Urban (thousands)	14.9	1.6	6.2	8.5	9.2	9.1	49.6
Rural (thousands)	2.6	3.6	9.3	9.8	10.5	14.7	50.4

table continues next page

Table A.9 Location of Employment in Multiple Ring Buffers from the Big Seven Cities (continued)

	Distance from the center						
	Fewer than 50 km	50–100 km	100–200 km	200–300 km	300–450 km	More than 450 km	Total
Agriculture, fishing, and mining							
National share (%)	4.8	10.3	21.9	24.1	20.2	18.8	100.0
Urban (thousands)	1.0	0.4	1.2	2.2	1.9	1.4	8.2
Rural (thousands)	3.8	9.8	20.7	21.9	18.2	17.4	91.8
Manufacturing							
National share (%)	19.3	5.1	17.0	18.9	18.0	21.8	100.0
Urban (thousands)	15.9	1.5	6.5	9.0	8.3	6.7	47.9
Rural (thousands)	3.4	3.6	10.4	9.9	9.8	15.0	52.1
Business services (transport, telecom, financial, real estate)							
National share (%)	29.2	4.1	12.9	16.8	19.7	17.3	100.0
Urban (thousands)	26.8	1.8	7.5	10.3	11.5	8.9	66.9
Rural (thousands)	2.4	2.3	5.4	6.5	8.1	8.3	33.1

Sources: Population censuses; Ministry of Statistics and Programme Implementation 2005.

Table A.10 Location of Manufacturing Industry in Multiple Ring Buffers from the Big Seven Cities

	Distance from the center						
	Fewer than 50 km	50–100 km	100–200 km	200–300 km	300–450 km	More than 450 km	Total
Manufacturing workers							
National share (%)	19.3	5.1	17.0	18.9	18.0	21.8	100.0
Urban (millions)	15.9	1.5	6.5	9.0	8.3	6.7	47.9
Rural (millions)	3.4	3.6	10.4	9.9	9.8	15.0	52.1
Low tech							
National share (%)	17.3	4.9	17.6	20.0	17.8	22.4	100.0
Urban (millions)	14.4	1.5	6.5	9.3	7.9	7.0	46.6
Rural (millions)	3.0	3.4	11.1	10.6	9.8	15.4	53.4
Medium low tech							
National share (%)	21.7	5.9	14.9	15.3	19.5	22.7	100.0
Urban (millions)	17.5	1.4	5.9	6.9	8.8	5.8	46.3
Rural (millions)	4.3	4.4	9.0	8.4	10.7	16.9	53.7
Medium high tech							
National share (%)	29.2	5.3	16.5	13.4	23.1	12.4	100.0
Urban (millions)	23.9	2.1	9.0	8.3	13.6	6.9	63.7
Rural (millions)	5.4	3.3	7.5	5.2	9.5	5.5	36.3
High tech							
National share (%)	35.7	8.8	27.1	11.4	11.4	5.7	100.0
Urban (millions)	25.6	2.1	17.6	3.7	6.2	3.2	58.4
Rural (millions)	10.0	6.6	9.5	7.7	5.2	2.5	41.6

table continues next page

Table A.10 Location of Manufacturing Industry in Multiple Ring Buffers from the Big Seven Cities (continued)

	Distance from the center						
	Fewer than 50 km	*50–100 km*	*100–200 km*	*200–300 km*	*300–450 km*	*More than 450 km*	*Total*
Fast-growing exports							
National share (%)	30.0	4.4	14.2	15.2	20.5	15.7	100.0
Urban (millions)	26.4	1.7	7.3	8.7	11.4	7.3	62.9
Rural (millions)	3.6	2.7	6.9	6.5	9.1	8.3	37.1
ICT services							
National share (%)	63.6	1.8	10.0	7.9	10.1	6.6	100.0
Urban (millions)	63.0	1.2	9.3	6.9	9.0	5.3	94.6
Rural (millions)	0.7	0.6	0.7	1.0	1.1	1.3	5.4

Source: Ministry of Statistics and Programme Implementation 2005.

Table A.11 Job Growth over 1998–2005 by Distance from the Big Seven Cities

percent

	Distance from seven largest cities						
	Fewer than 50 km	*50–100 km*	*100–200 km*	*200–300 km*	*300–450 km*	*More than 450 km*	*Total*
Total employment	13.1	16.9	25.1	32.0	21.7	17.3	21.3
Agriculture, hunting, and forestry	0.5	8.5	64.2	130.3	80.9	65.6	67.0
Manufacturing	−2.7	1.0	5.8	16.4	9.5	2.8	5.6
Fast-growing exports	−10.3	23.8	8.9	25.6	15.4	17.6	7.4
Low tech	15.7	−8.9	11.7	23.0	19.5	3.8	12.5
Medium low tech	−18.1	11.4	−1.0	6.1	−2.0	−2.6	−3.5
Medium high tech	−22.7	49.3	−11.4	6.9	−8.3	21.1	−7.3
High tech	−10.5	41.0	−25.3	−34.6	2.7	−6.8	−14.6
Construction	−2.6	−28.6	−4.0	−3.2	2.3	−15.3	−6.1
Transport, storage, and communications	10.3	64.4	39.7	43.7	23.9	1.2	23.9
Financial intermediation	−5.6	15.0	18.9	27.3	28.4	−1.1	11.8
Real estate, renting, and business activities	117.2	90.5	90.0	92.2	67.4	48.7	87.4
Education	64.9	45.5	46.1	39.4	32.9	22.8	37.0
ICT services	390.0	270.8	413.2	330.6	377.5	383.0	383.7

Sources: Ministry of Statistics and Programme Implementation 1998 and 2005.

Table A.12 Job Growth over 1998–2005 by Distance from the Big Seven Cities: The North versus the South
percent

| | Distance from seven largest cities | | | | | | |
	Fewer than 50 km	50–100 km	100–200 km	200–300 km	300–450 km	More than 450 km	Total
Total employment							
North	6.9	17.3	19.9	19.6	16.7	11.6	14.6
South	55.5	12.3	32.6	52.2	31.7	45.6	39.9
Agriculture, hunting, and forestry							
North	12.0	22.3	100.3	74.2	39.3	31.2	47.0
South	−14.5	−5.8	54.8	228.9	217.3	150.7	107.3
Manufacturing							
North	−10.7	2.9	1.1	12.4	8.2	3.8	1.8
South	39.7	−9.1	12.9	25.5	15.6	9.5	17.3
Fast-growing exports							
North	−21.4	23.3	−3.8	−1.9	7.9	3.1	−6.8
South	36.1	34.5	58.0	79.0	26.9	97.3	48.2
Low tech							
North	10.7	−2.2	8.3	31.1	14.9	5.7	11.5
South	64.4	−26.5	8.3	19.7	23.7	5.0	14.3
Medium low tech							
North	−28.0	4.7	−2.7	−5.9	2.8	−2.6	−7.9
South	20.4	40.2	31.7	44.3	1.4	32.9	25.6
Medium high tech							
North	−35.5	42.6	−18.7	−6.0	−7.9	24.6	−15.8
South	26.8	109.0	76.9	53.8	1.1	37.8	27.6
High tech							
North	−7.6	49.6	−47.7	−49.6	−6.7	37.0	−29.5
South	−22.6	54.9	154.8	99.4	48.6	−2.0	7.8
Construction							
North	−39.9	−50.4	−17.3	−18.9	−13.9	−24.1	−24.7
South	68.6	6.5	18.5	28.3	41.2	117.5	39.8
Transport, storage and communications							
North	14.8	59.5	19.6	17.1	3.8	−30.5	7.3
South	81.3	119.0	95.8	86.7	59.5	55.3	77.7
Financial intermediation							
North	3.8	11.9	12.8	5.7	6.4	−19.7	1.6
South	33.1	17.3	21.1	31.7	31.0	48.1	30.8
Real estate, renting and business activities							
North	99.3	97.8	73.5	84.7	34.3	24.2	65.0
South	213.3	64.4	73.9	119.3	109.3	183.9	138.7

table continues next page

Table A.12 Job Growth over 1998–2005 by Distance from the Big Seven Cities: The North versus the South
(continued)

	Distance from seven largest cities						
	Fewer than 50 km	*50–100 km*	*100–200 km*	*200–300 km*	*300–450 km*	*More than 450 km*	*Total*
Education							
North	97.5	42.0	33.6	30.5	27.8	18.8	32.6
South	61.0	47.3	58.2	49.6	42.2	80.1	53.7
ICT services							
North	305.5	669.0	334.4	314.2	217.8	426.4	313.9
South	389.7	37.4	285.2	366.3	550.3	325.2	383.3

Sources: Ministry of Statistics and Programme Implementation 1998 and 2005.

Table A.13 Changes in National Employment Shares over 1998–2005 by Distance from the Big Seven Cities: Delhi, Mumbai, and Chennai-Hyderabad-Bangalore
percentage points

	Distance from seven largest cities						
	Fewer than 50 km	*50–100 km*	*100–200 km*	*200–300 km*	*300–450 km*	*More than 450 km*	*Total*
Total employment							
Delhi	−0.5	0.1	0.0	0.1	−0.1	−0.2	−0.6
Mumbai	−1.3	0.0	0.1	−0.2	−0.2	0.0	−1.6
Chennai-Hyderabad-Bangalore	1.1	−0.2	0.6	1.4	0.2	0.3	3.5
Manufacturing							
Delhi	−1.4	0.1	−0.3	−0.1	−0.1	−0.5	−2.3
Mumbai	−0.8	0.0	−0.2	−0.3	−0.3	−0.1	−1.7
Chennai-Hyderabad-Bangalore	1.0	−0.3	0.5	1.1	0.2	0.0	2.6
Fast-growing exports							
Delhi	−3.5	0.2	−0.5	−0.5	0.0	0.0	−4.4
Mumbai	−1.4	0.1	−0.9	0.6	−0.4	0.0	−1.9
Chennai-Hyderabad-Bangalore	1.5	0.3	1.5	1.8	0.2	0.6	5.9
Low tech							
Delhi	−0.8	−0.1	0.0	0.2	−0.1	−0.8	−1.6
Mumbai	−0.6	−0.1	0.5	−0.4	0.2	−0.2	−0.5
Chennai-Hyderabad-Bangalore	1.1	−1.0	−0.3	0.4	0.2	−0.4	−0.1
Medium low tech							
Delhi	−1.3	0.4	−0.5	−0.3	−0.1	−0.4	−2.1
Mumbai	−0.6	0.2	−0.8	−0.1	−0.8	−0.1	−2.1
Chennai-Hyderabad-Bangalore	0.9	0.5	1.1	2.0	0.3	0.6	5.3
Medium high tech							
Delhi	−3.1	0.4	−0.8	−1.0	0.2	0.5	−3.8
Mumbai	−2.1	0.5	−2.0	0.3	−2.0	0.0	−5.4
Chennai-Hyderabad-Bangalore	2.4	1.3	1.7	1.4	0.3	0.4	7.6

table continues next page

Table A.13 Changes in National Employment Shares over 1998–2005 by Distance from the Big Seven Cities: Delhi, Mumbai, and Chennai-Hyderabad-Bangalore *(continued)*

	Distance from seven largest cities						
	Fewer than 50 km	*50–100 km*	*100–200 km*	*200–300 km*	*300–450 km*	*More than 450 km*	*Total*
High tech							
Delhi	−1.2	0.4	−11.2	−7.1	0.0	0.0	−19.2
Mumbai	1.9	1.5	4.2	0.3	−0.1	−0.1	7.6
Chennai-Hyderabad-Bangalore	−1.2	2.2	0.6	0.7	0.9	0.3	3.5
ICT services							
Delhi	−1.9	0.2	−0.3	−0.1	−0.3	0.2	−2.3
Mumbai	3.6	0.0	1.6	−0.2	−0.2	0.1	4.8
Chennai-Hyderabad-Bangalore	0.4	−0.9	−0.9	−0.4	0.1	−0.3	−2.0

Sources: Ministry of Statistics and Programme Implementation 1998 and 2005.
Note: Delhi comprises Delhi, Haryana, and Uttar Pradesh; Mumbai comprises Maharashtra and Gujarat; and Chennai-Hyderabad-Bangalore comprises Tamil Nadu, Andhra Pradesh, and Karnataka.

Table A.14 Location of Job Growth in Multiple Ring Buffers around Large Cities, 1998–2005
percent

		Distance from city center						
		Less than 25 km	*25–50 km*	*50–100 km*	*100–150 km*	*150–200 km*	*More than 200 km*	*Total*
All employment	National, from 7 largest cities	1.4	3.1	1.8	2.4	3.7	2.9	2.7
	Karnataka, from Bangalore	3.4	2.2	0.5	1.7	4.3	2.8	2.7
	Tamil Nadu, from Chennai	5.8	9.0	3.1	4.1	5.5	4.7	4.9
ICT services	National	24.6	29.3	18.9	24.9	21.4	20.0	22.5
	Karnataka	24.6	39.1	38.9	9.8	30.0	23.4	24.4
	Tamil Nadu	26.7	46.5	8.7	18.2	20.7	16.9	22.9
Manufacturing	National	−2.4	1.5	−0.4	−0.6	1.4	1.5	0.8
	Karnataka	2.9	5.5	1.8	−0.1	1.8	2.7	2.5
	Tamil Nadu	0.4	12.1	−1.2	0.7	3.4	1.7	2.0
Low tech	National	1.6	0.8	−1.6	0.1	2.3	2.1	1.7
	Karnataka	2.0	−0.4	1.4	−1.3	2.0	3.5	2.4
	Tamil Nadu	5.8	16.3	−6.8	−0.7	2.5	0.7	1.0
Medium low tech	National	−5.6	0.3	1.0	−1.7	0.4	0.4	−0.5
	Karnataka	4.2	10.8	−0.8	1.0	0.0	0.6	1.9
	Tamil Nadu	−0.6	5.1	10.6	4.2	9.6	6.0	5.4
Medium high tech	National	−7.4	4.8	5.1	−1.8	−2.8	0.7	−1.1
	Karnataka	4.0	21.9	15.4	12.4	1.0	−2.8	4.4
	Tamil Nadu	−7.5	16.2	7.2	12.9	3.9	2.2	2.7
High tech	National	−10.0	14.4	5.4	−0.5	−8.0	−1.6	−2.3
	Karnataka	1.1	73.2	52.0	15.0	−18.6	12.9	12.2
	Tamil Nadu	−24.5	23.3	8.0	31.6	32.0	21.2	10.6

table continues next page

Table A.14 Location of Job Growth in Multiple Ring Buffers around Large Cities, 1998–2005 *(continued)*

		Distance from city center						
		Less than 25 km	25–50 km	50–100 km	100–150 km	150–200 km	More than 200 km	Total
High-export growth	National	−4.0	4.5	2.7	0.4	1.5	2.6	1.0
	Karnataka	2.4	17.5	3.1	4.1	5.9	0.7	3.0
	Tamil Nadu	−3.5	17.0	4.4	8.5	7.0	4.1	4.2
Construction	National	−4.8	0.3	−6.0	−1.9	1.3	−0.3	−0.9
	Karnataka	−5.6	5.0	−8.2	1.4	−2.6	0.5	−1.2
	Tamil Nadu	6.9	26.8	−0.5	3.5	7.2	4.4	5.6
Wholesale and retail trade	National	3.4	4.9	2.8	3.8	4.3	3.8	3.7
	Karnataka	−0.1	3.5	1.4	4.1	2.2	0.6	1.1
	Tamil Nadu	5.5	7.5	1.3	1.2	1.5	1.8	2.5
Transport, storage, and communications	National	0.5	9.1	6.4	3.9	5.9	2.5	3.1
	Karnataka	−0.2	−0.7	5.6	3.7	5.5	7.6	5.2
	Tamil Nadu	7.4	10.7	4.6	3.1	11.4	8.0	7.9
Education	National	8.9	7.7	5.2	5.3	5.3	3.9	4.5
	Karnataka	5.5	4.5	3.8	5.4	4.6	7.1	6.0
	Tamil Nadu	5.2	3.8	1.1	3.2	8.3	5.9	5.6
Health and social work	National	6.0	4.5	1.9	3.8	4.5	2.6	3.2
	Karnataka	10.1	16.1	4.6	9.5	7.4	5.9	7.3
	Tamil Nadu	10.2	3.4	1.5	6.0	9.4	5.0	6.3

Sources: Ministry of Statistics and Programme Implementation 1998 and 2005.

Table A.15 Industrial Specialization in India: Location Quotient by Activity and City Size
location quotient

	City sizes					
	More than 4 million	1–4 million	100,000–1 million	50,000–100,000	20,000–50,000	Fewer than 20,000
Agriculture and forestry	0.27	0.80	1.04	1.54	1.74	2.14
Fishing	0.26	0.37	1.33	1.73	1.18	2.47
Mining and quarrying	0.52	1.02	1.06	1.10	1.20	2.20
Manufacturing	1.06	1.15	0.94	0.96	0.93	0.88
Low-tech	1.01	1.06	0.97	1.04	0.99	0.94
Medium low-tech	1.18	1.30	0.89	0.77	0.79	0.79
Medium high-tech	1.13	1.60	0.77	0.94	0.77	0.70
High-tech	1.39	1.41	0.69	0.62	1.00	0.48
Fast-growing exports	1.33	1.17	0.81	0.88	0.75	0.77
ICT services	2.09	1.00	0.71	0.27	0.27	0.19
Utilities (electricity, gas, and water)	0.90	0.84	0.95	1.04	1.17	1.61
Construction	0.99	1.04	1.10	0.93	0.84	0.89
Wholesale and retail	0.99	0.96	1.00	1.02	1.05	1.04

table continues next page

Table A.15 Industrial Specialization in India: Location Quotient by Activity and City Size (continued)

	City sizes					
	More than 4 million	1–4 million	100,000–1 million	50,000–100,000	20,000–50,000	Fewer than 20,000
Hotels and restaurants	0.96	0.92	1.00	1.02	1.09	1.11
Transport and telecom	1.23	0.94	0.98	0.87	0.83	0.75
Financial services	1.16	1.02	1.02	0.88	0.82	0.73
Real estate	1.65	0.97	0.79	0.67	0.60	0.54
Public administration	0.64	0.93	1.21	1.21	1.17	1.10
Education	0.85	0.97	1.06	1.01	1.08	1.25
Health and social work	1.02	1.08	1.06	0.91	0.85	0.88
Other services	1.01	0.92	0.98	1.01	1.06	1.08

Source: Urban Development and Local Government Unit, World Bank, based on Ministry of Statistics and Programme Implementation 2005.

Table A.16 Industrial Specialization in China, the United States, and Brazil, 2000
location quotient

	City size				
China	1 (more than 4 million)	2 (2.5–4 million)	3 (1.5–2.5 million)	4 (1–1.5 million)	5 (less than 1 million)
Agriculture	0.53	0.54	0.97	1.18	1.71
Mining	0.29	0.50	1.05	1.59	1.65
Manufacturing	1.30	1.49	0.94	0.86	0.49
Utilities (power, gas, and water)	0.81	0.86	1.26	1.26	0.95
Construction	1.19	1.08	1.12	0.95	0.71
Transportation and telecom	1.08	0.99	1.07	1.03	0.85
Wholesale and resale trade	1.25	1.16	1.03	0.89	0.68
Finance and insurance	1.07	1.12	1.09	0.99	0.79
Real estate	1.91	0.96	0.81	0.73	0.39
Social services	1.46	1.08	0.96	0.82	0.62
Health	1.10	1.02	1.12	0.97	0.83
Education	1.16	1.06	1.07	0.91	0.81
Scientific research	1.78	1.24	1.03	0.48	0.36
Government agencies	0.97	1.01	1.09	1.05	0.93

Source: Urban Development and Local Government Unit, World Bank.

United States	Large cities	Medium cities	Small cities	Rural
Agriculture	0.16	0.34	0.91	2.60
Manufacturing	0.76	0.93	1.13	1.18
Transport, storage, and communications	1.31	1.03	0.93	0.73
Financial services	1.33	1.13	0.92	0.62
Real estate	1.31	1.12	0.90	0.67
Public administration and social security	0.86	0.89	1.04	1.22

table continues next page

Table A.16 Industrial Specialization in China, the United States, and Brazil, 2000 (continued)

United States	Large cities	Medium cities	Small cities	Rural
Education	1.40	0.98	0.94	0.68
Health	0.99	0.96	1.01	1.04

Source: Holmes and Stevens 2004.

	City size			
Brazil	More than 4 million	1–4 million	100,000–1 million	50,000–100,000
Agriculture	0.55	0.84	1.66	2.66
Manufacturing	1.05	0.92	1.01	0.89
Transport, storage, and communications	1.15	0.98	0.83	0.74
Financial services	1.41	0.88	0.60	0.42
Public administration and social security	0.86	1.20	0.99	1.05
Education	0.96	1.04	1.02	0.95
Health	1.14	0.99	0.85	0.74

Source: Urban Development and Local Government Unit, World Bank using data from Da Mata and others 2007.

References

Da Mata, Daniel, Uri Deichmann, J. Vernon Henderson, Somik Lall, and H. G. Wang. 2007. "Determinant of City Growth in Brazil." *Journal of Urban Economics* 62 (2): 252–72.

Holmes, Thomas J., and John J. Stevens. 2004. "Spatial Distribution of Economic Activities in North America." In *Handbook of Regional and Urban Economics, vol. 4, Cities and Geography*, edited by J. Vernon Henderson and Jacques-François Thisse, 2797–843. Amsterdam: North-Holland.

Ministry of Home Affairs. 1991. *Census of India 1991*. Office of the Registrar General and Census Commissioner, New Delhi.

———. 2001. *Census of India: Census Data 2001*. Office of the Registrar General and Census Commissioner, New Delhi.

———. 2011. *Census of India 2011*. Office of the Registrar General and Census Commissioner, New Delhi.

Ministry of Statistics and Programme Implementation. 1998. *Economic Census 1998: All India Report*. Central Statistical Organisation, New Delhi.

———. 2005. *Provisional Results of Economic Census 2005: All India Report*. Central Statistical Organisation, New Delhi.

Data Sources and Methodology for Tables and Maps

The main sources of socioeconomic data used in the analysis in chapter 2 are the population censuses up to 2001 and the 1998 and 2005 economic censuses. The population census data are aggregated at the town level for urban populations and at the tehsil level for rural populations.[1] The economic census data were processed and aggregated at the same town and tehsil levels as the 2001 population census, and then linked, allowing socioeconomic trends to be assessed systematically.

The combined socioeconomic data were then geo-referenced to identify the location of towns and tehsils and their geographic proximity to the different levels of urban cores, such as the urban centers (largest population towns) in an urban agglomeration (UA), and with more than 100,000, 500,000, 1 million, 4 million, or 7 million people (as of 2001). This exercise revealed the nature of rural economic activities in urban fringe areas closer to big cities, and more important, the different spatial profiles of industrial specialization that benefit from increasing returns to scale.

To group India's urban system for descriptive typology analysis, towns in the same UA were aggregated to generate UA and non-UA town data. The 2001 UA definitions from the Census Office, which includes 384 UAs (covering 1,167 towns) and 3,994 non-UA towns, were used. Those UAs and non-UA towns following the official city size classification were then grouped: class 1 (IA) more than 4 million, class 2 (IB) 1–4 million, class 3 (IC) 100,000–1 million, class 4 (II) 50,000–100,000, class 5 (III) 20,000–50,000, and class 6 (IV+) fewer than 20,000. The 2001 definition of 4,378 UA and towns was back-cast to different years to construct a time-consistent panel dataset.

The economic census collects employment data on establishments of all sizes and sectors. Our analysis of these data is at a uniquely high level of spatial detail— villages for rural areas, and towns for urban areas (see table A5). By linking towns and villages with their centroid locations, and matching the village and town identifiers across 1998 and 2005, we can identify changes in employment patterns in and near cities and towns at high spatial resolution; for example, we can distinguish between employment growth in city cores and in rings 10–50 km around the cores.

The spatial analysis also drew on two rounds of the Annual Survey of Industries (ASI), 1993 and 2006 (Ministry of Statistics and Programme Implementation 1994 and 2007). The ASI covers formal manufacturing establishments; specifically, it is a representative survey of "factories," where a factory is defined as a manufacturing establishment that employs 10 workers or more if it uses power, or 20 workers or more if it does not use power. The ASI sector accounts for more than 80 percent of all manufacturing fixed capital in India, but less than 20 percent of all manufacturing employment. Although the ASI covers a subset of the establishments captured in the economic census, it is more regular, available over a longer period, and contains information not just on employment but also fixed capital (plant and machinery), outputs, and inputs.

While we would have liked to analyze ASI data at the same high level of spatial detail as the economic census, the district level was the best possible, because the ASI does not provide any other spatial identifiers. To examine trends by city size in the ASI, we categorized districts based on the size of their nearest major city. Districts in the Metro category are those within 100 km of the largest seven metropolitan areas (with more than 4 million people as of 2001). This category includes 23 districts: Delhi, Mumbai, Kolkata, Chennai, Bangalore, Hyderabad, Ahmedabad, and their surrounding districts. Next, the category "Million Plus" contains those districts whose nearest major city (within 50 km) has a population of 1–4 million (excluding the "Metro" districts). The next category contains districts whose nearest major city (within 50 km) is a Class 3 city with a population of 100,000 to 1 million. The last category contains all other districts.

Note

1. A tehsil represents an administrative subdivision or tier of local government of nearly 100–350 villages in India (Malhotra, Chariar, and Das 2009).

References

Malhotra, Charru, V. M. Chariar, and L. K. Das. 2009. "ICT and Societal Concerns at the Grassroots: TARAhaat Experience in Rural Areas of *Tikamgarh* District of Madhya Pradesh in India." In *E-Governance in Practice*, 224–39, edited by H. M. Chawla. GIFT Publishing-IK Books.

Ministry of Statistics and Programme Implementation. 1994. *Annual Survey of Industries 1993–94*. New Delhi.

———. 2007. *Annual Survey of Industries 2006*. New Delhi.

APPENDIX C

Results from a Survey of Truckers

Table C.1 Trucking Price and Cost Structure by City Size and Route Type

	Big cities (more than 4 million)		Others (fewer than 4 million)		
	Intra-urban (fewer than 100 km)	Extra-urban (more than 100 km)	Intra-urban (fewer than 100 km)	Extra-urban (more than 100 km)	Total
Price charged per ton km (Rs)	5.2	2.5	4.5	2.0	2.6
a. Relative to national average	201.5	95.6	176.7	79.2	100.0
Total costs per ton km (Rs)	4.7	2.7	5.7	3.0	3.0
b. Relative to national average	159.2	90.1	191.7	102.1	100.0
(a–b)	42.3	5.5	−15.0	−22.9	0.0
Share to total costs (%)					
Fuel	54.1	69.4	59.9	73.6	70.2
Salary	14.0	5.6	9.8	5.2	5.6
Route allowance	7.7	4.4	7.7	4.3	4.4
Maintenance	8.8	6.6	8.9	6.1	6.5
Official overhead costs (tolls, road taxes)	9.8	9.6	7.4	6.6	8.8
Unofficial overhead costs (informal facilitation payments)	5.6	4.4	6.3	4.3	4.4

Source: Based on a survey report for the World Bank by the Nielsen Consulting Company in 2010.

Table C.2 List of Trucking Survey Cities and Routes

Surveyed cities	Trucks' operation (coming from or going to)		
	Metro	Neighborhood urban (within state)	Neighborhood rural (within state)
Delhi	Mumbai	Ambala	Hapur
Ahmedabad	Mumbai	Kandla	Mahesana
Chandigarh	Delhi	Jullunder	Ferozpur
Mumbai	Bangalore	Pune	Baramati
Chennai	Kolkata	Coimbatore	Vellore
Hyderabad	Chennai	Vijawada	Mahaboobnagar
Bangalore	Chennai	Mangalore	Tumkur
Bhopal	Mumbai	Indore	Satna
Kolkata	Delhi	Ranchi	Midnapur
Trivandrum	Chennai	Cochin	Kollam
Patna	Kolkata	Ranchi	Darbhanga
Guwahati	Kolkata	Jorhat	Jagiroad
Varanasi	Delhi	Lucknow	Mirzapur
Bhuvaneshwar	Kolkata	Sambalpur	Puri
Panji	Mumbai	Kolhapur	Karwar

Source: Based on a survey report for the World Bank by the Nielsen Consulting Company in 2010.

Table C.3 Factors Determining the Unit Price of Intra-Urban Freight Movements

Dependent variable	(1)	(2)	(3)	(4)
	Ln(Price charged, per ton km, Rs), within 100 km trip distance			
Ln(one trip distance, round trip, km)	−0.588*	−0.608**	−0.561*	−0.572*
	(0.242)	(0.234)	(0.256)	(0.245)
Ln(truck utilization [yearly mileage, km])		−0.042***		−0.042***
		(0.008)		(0.008)
Ratio of empty backhaul			−0.023	−0.031
			(0.034)	(0.028)
Constant	Yes	Yes	Yes	Yes
Observations	211	211	211	211
R-squared	0.196	0.267	0.200	0.273

Source: Based on a survey report for the World Bank by the Nielsen Consulting Company in 2010.
Note: Ordinary least squares regressions use robust cluster standard errors. Numbers in parenthesis represent robust standard errors. We assume the observations may be correlated within routes, but would be independent between routes.
Significance level: * = 10%, ** = 5%, *** = 1%.

www.ingramcontent.com/pod-product-compliance
Lightning Source LLC
Chambersburg PA
CBHW080618270326
41928CB00016B/3108